Stephanie Alexander

For 21 years from 1976, Stephanie Alexander was the force behind Stephanie's restaurant in Hawthorn, a landmark establishment credited with having revolutionised fine dining in Melbourne. From 1997 to 2005 Stephanie, along with several friends, owned the Richmond Hill Café and Larder, a neighbourhood restaurant renowned for its specialist cheese retailing. In her recently published memoir, *A Cook's Life*, she recounts how her uncompromising dedication to good food has shaped her life and changed the eating habits of a nation.

One of Australia's most highly acclaimed food authors, Stephanie has written fourteen books, including *Stephanie's Menus for Food Lovers*, *Stephanie Alexander's Kitchen Garden Companion* and *Stephanie Alexander & Maggie Beer's Tuscan Cookbook* (co-author). Her signature publication, *The Cook's Companion*, has established itself as the kitchen bible in over 500 000 homes. With characteristic determination, in 2001 Stephanie initiated the Kitchen Garden at Collingwood College in order to allow young children to experience the very things that made her own childhood so rich: the growing, harvesting, cooking and sharing of good food.

Visit Stephanie Alexander online at stephaniealexander.com.au

LANTERN COOKERY CLASSICS

Stephanie Alexander

LANTERN
an imprint of
PENGUIN BOOKS

STARTERS, SOUPS AND SIDES

MAINS

SWEETS

BASICS

Starters, soups and sides

Apple and bacon salad with quail eggs and hazelnuts

This is the sort of starter I love. It has plenty of interest in terms of both flavour and texture but is not too filling, leaving you with an appetite for the next course. I find it easiest to saw each quail egg shell gently with a serrated knife until you break through the shell and then slide the tiny egg into a small bowl.

50 g hazelnuts or walnuts
8 quail eggs
2 crisp eating apples, cored, quartered and
    cut into thin pieces
juice of ½ lemon
250 g green beans, as small and tender
    as possible, trimmed
salt
100 g rindless smoked streaky bacon or
    thin slices pancetta, cut into
    1 cm-wide strips
4 small handfuls tender rocket leaves,
    washed and dried
4 small handfuls other tender salad leaves,
    washed and dried

DRESSING
¼ cup (60 ml) extra-virgin olive oil
1 tablespoon hazelnut or walnut oil
2 teaspoons red-wine vinegar
sea salt and freshly ground
    black pepper

1 Preheat oven to 150°C. Put nuts on a baking tray and roast for 8 minutes or until golden. If using hazelnuts, rub hard in a dry tea towel to remove most of the skins, then pick nuts from debris and set aside until needed. Gently cut through end of each quail shell and slide each egg into its own small bowl. Place apple in a bowl and drizzle with lemon juice.

2 To make the dressing, whisk together all ingredients and taste for salt and pepper. Reserve until needed.

3 Cook green beans in a saucepan of simmering salted water for 5 minutes or until bite-tender. Drain and transfer to bowl of dressing.

4 Sauté bacon or pancetta in a non-stick frying pan over low heat, stirring until crisp. Transfer to an ovenproof bowl and keep warm in the oven. Immediately slide quail eggs into the hot frying pan and cook for 1 minute or until set. Put salad greens into a large bowl and scatter over bacon or pancetta, apple and nuts. Add green beans and dressing. Mix with your hands. Taste for seasoning.

5 Divide salad among 4 bowls or plates. Slip 2 quail eggs on top of each salad and serve.

Stephanie's everyday salad vinaigrette

I always make my vinaigrette directly in the salad bowl as it saves fiddling around with small bowls. I cross the salad servers over the dressing, then pile the washed and dried leaves on top and transfer the bowl to the refrigerator until it is time to serve the salad. When it is brought to the table the salad servers are pulled away so that the leaves sink down into the bowl and are then tossed gently but thoroughly. Simple! After a few goes you will not need the measuring spoons, but will be comfortable estimating the quantities of vinegar and olive oil. Every cook has a few obsessions: mine is a dislike of balsamic vinegar in a classic green salad. I find the sweetness quite inappropriate.

a pinch sea salt
1 teaspoon red-wine or sherry vinegar
freshly ground black pepper
1 tablespoon best-quality extra-virgin olive oil
4–6 handfuls washed and dried salad leaves

Extra bits for salads
This is a list of some of the garnishes that can be added to leafy salads. I am sure there are many more I have not thought of.

avocado chunks
bacon fried with a trace of oil until crisp,
    drained on paper towel and crumbled
bread croutons, tossed in oil and fried or
    baked until golden and crisp
caramelised onion
crumbled blue cheese
cubes of Gruyère-style cheese
flaked almonds fried in butter until golden
    and drained on paper towel
fried quail eggs
marinated goat's cheese
toasted pumpkin or sunflower seeds

1 Sprinkle salt into a salad bowl, crumbling it as you do so, then add vinegar. Stir with one of the salad servers to dissolve salt. Grind on pepper and add olive oil. Taste for balance of salt and acid. Put salad servers in the bowl, crossed over to form a barrier.

2 Add salad leaves and refrigerate until needed. Remove salad servers and toss, then serve at once.

Raw mushroom, rocket and bread salad

This salad is a favourite of mine. Raw mushrooms have an unusual nutty flavour that combines wonderfully with rocket and the slightly salty cheese, ricotta salata. This pressed and salted style of ricotta is not easy to find, so you should head to a delicatessen that is patronised by Italians. If it is not obtainable, substitute pecorino or even parmesan. However, parmesan is a bit aristocratic (and much more expensive) for what is really a pretty rustic salad.

2 slices sourdough bread, crusts
    removed (about 100 g)
150 ml extra-virgin olive oil,
    plus extra for drizzling
1 clove garlic, halved
300 g button mushrooms, bases
    trimmed and caps thinly sliced
100 g shaved ricotta salata (see
    page 140) or pecorino
sea salt and freshly ground
    black pepper
1 tablespoon lemon juice
4 handfuls rocket leaves,
    washed and dried

1 Brush bread slices with 1 tablespoon of the olive oil and toast in a dry large non-stick frying pan over medium heat, turning after 3 minutes, until both sides have taken colour and look crisp. Transfer bread to a plate, then rub lightly with cut garlic. When cool enough to handle, cut into 1 cm cubes and drop into a salad bowl. Add mushrooms, cheese, salt and pepper to the bowl, then drizzle over lemon juice and remaining olive oil.

2 Turn salad over and over with a large spoon and then leave for about 10 minutes to allow flavours to mellow and mushrooms to soften. Taste a mushroom slice for salt and pepper and adjust seasoning if desired.

3 At the last minute, toss rocket leaves through salad and serve. An extra drizzle of olive oil may be a good idea.

Zucchini flowers with mortadella and bread stuffing

This stuffing for zucchini flowers includes delicately flavoured and smoothly textured mortadella.

½ cup (35 g) fresh breadcrumbs
1 tablespoon water
100 g mortadella, coarsely chopped
1 clove garlic, finely chopped
2 tablespoons chopped flat-leaf parsley
25 g parmesan, grated
1 tablespoon extra-virgin olive oil
sea salt and freshly ground black pepper
12 male zucchini flowers, stamens
    removed (optional)
vegetable or olive oil, for deep-frying
1 quantity Beer Batter (see page 137) or
    Eggwhite Batter (see page 137)

1 Put breadcrumbs and water into a mixing bowl and leave for 10 minutes. Finely chop mortadella in a food processor. Scrape into bowl with breadcrumbs and add garlic, parsley, parmesan and olive oil. Season with salt and pepper.

2 Preheat oven to 100°C and put a baking tray lined thickly with paper towel inside to keep warm.

3 Put a spoonful of mortadella and bread stuffing into each zucchini flower and gently fold petals around filling. Twirl petal ends to seal.

4 Pour oil into a large non-stick frying pan or a wok to a depth of 1.5 cm in the centre, then heat over high heat until hot. Test oil with a drop of batter; it should sizzle and turn golden almost immediately. Working in batches, dip stuffed flowers into batter, drain off excess and carefully place in hot oil; don't crowd the pan. Turn fritters to brown other side. Lift out with tongs, allowing excess oil to drain into the pan. Place on a baking tray and keep warm in oven until all zucchini flowers are fried. Serve at once.

Salmon patties with dill

Here fresh salmon is combined with dill and used to make light patties that are lovely served with waxy potatoes tossed while hot with dill-flavoured sour cream. For a party, tiny patties can be served on toothpicks with either dill-flavoured sour cream for dipping or topped with a dollop of the mayonnaise on page 137 and a sprig of dill, as I've done here.

1 × 300 g salmon fillet, skin removed and
   pin-boned (ask your fishmonger to do this)
2 tablespoons thickened cream
30 g fresh breadcrumbs (from about
   1 thick slice bread)
30 g marinated goat's cheese
1 free-range egg yolk
¼ cup (3 tablespoons) chopped dill
½ teaspoon sea salt
freshly ground black pepper
2 tablespoons plain flour
20 g butter
2 tablespoons olive oil

1 Cut salmon into bite-sized pieces. Pour cream over breadcrumbs and leave for 5 minutes.

2 Process salmon, cream-soaked crumbs and goat's cheese in a food processor; do this quickly as you want it all combined but not reduced to a paste. Scrape mixture into a mixing bowl and mix in egg yolk and dill, then season with salt and pepper to taste. (Fry a tiny ball of the mixture to check the salt and pepper if you can't bring yourself to taste it raw.) Cover mixture with plastic film and chill in refrigerator for 30 minutes. Dampen your hands and divide mixture into 8 large or 24 bite-sized patties. Roll each one in flour.

3 Heat butter and olive oil in a large non-stick frying pan over medium heat and fry patties for 2–3 minutes per side or until golden brown. (Don't cook too long as salmon cooks very fast and is much nicer if still moist.) Serve at once.

Fresh mozzarella, bread and oregano skewers with anchovy sauce

These can be made very small for hand-around snacks or a little larger to be served on a bed of inner cos leaves or baby spinach (either raw or just wilted), to serve as a simple starter.

4 thick slices day-old bread (from a sourdough or other substantial loaf), crusts removed
extra-virgin olive oil, for brushing
8 × 10 cm-long oregano sprigs, plus extra oregano, chopped
4 balls fresh mozzarella (see page 140), cut into 4–6 pieces depending on size
60 g unsalted butter, melted
4 handfuls inner cos or baby spinach leaves (optional)

ANCHOVY SAUCE
100 ml pouring cream
1 clove garlic, chopped
a tiny pinch salt
20 g unsalted butter
4 anchovy fillets, chopped
1 teaspoon finely chopped flat-leaf parsley
1 tablespoon finely chopped oregano

1 To make the anchovy sauce, boil cream in a small saucepan over medium heat, stirring for 2 minutes until it has thickened and reduced a little. Set aside. Pound garlic and salt with a mortar and pestle to make a paste, then transfer to a small non-stick frying pan. Add butter and anchovy. Stir together over low heat until anchovy has dissolved. Stir in cream, parsley and oregano and set aside.

2 Line a griller tray with foil, then preheat griller. Lightly brush bread with olive oil and toast in a dry non-stick frying pan over medium heat until it starts to colour, then tear or cut each slice into very rough 2 cm pieces. Tie 2 oregano sprigs onto each skewer (or tear sprigs into smaller pieces and push into each piece of cheese). Slip pieces of bread and cheese onto skewers, starting and finishing with bread. Balance skewers across a baking tray or heatproof platter so that bread doesn't touch the bottom. Brush all sides with melted butter and scatter over chopped oregano.

3 Grill skewers for 2 minutes per side or until cheese just starts to soften and edges of oiled bread are just starting to toast.

4 Serve as hand-around snacks, drizzled with a little anchovy sauce. If serving as a starter you might want to place skewers on top of some inner cos or baby spinach leaves on each plate and drizzle with sauce.

Fritto misto of sage leaf fritters, fish, zucchini and prawns

SERVES 4

Almost everyone loves deep-fried food (but not indulging in it too often has to be the message). It's important to be mindful of offering a balance in the rest of the meal. I suggest following this with something fresh or crunchy, such as a leafy green salad. When preparing the sage leaf fritters (pictured right), retain a bit of stalk to help lift them in and out of the batter.

The safe leaf fritters alone make a great snack to serve with aperitifs.

5 anchovy fillets, halved lengthways
20 large sage leaves
1 free-range egg white, lightly whisked
    with a fork to break the gel
vegetable oil, for deep-frying
1 quantity Beer Batter (see page 137)
4 raw prawns, heads and tails removed
    and de-veined
4 fillets bone-free white fish, such as
    flathead tails or King George whiting
2–4 small zucchini (courgettes), cut
    lengthways into 2–3 slices
4 zucchini (courgette) flowers (optional)
½ cup other small pieces of vegetable
    (such as broccoli or cauliflower florets)
sea salt
lemon wedges, to serve

1 Preheat oven to 100°C and put a baking tray thickly lined with paper towel inside to keep warm.

2 Brush sage leaves with a very little egg white, then sandwich an anchovy piece between 2 sage leaves and press together lightly. Repeat with remaining anchovies and sage. Pour vegetable oil into a wok or deep-sided frying pan to a depth of 4 cm in the centre and heat over high heat until hot. Test oil with a drop of batter; it should sizzle and turn golden almost immediately. Dip fritters into batter, drain off excess and carefully place into hot oil; don't crowd the pan. Turn fritters to brown other side. Lift fritters out with a skimmer or slotted spoon, allowing excess oil to drain into the pan. Place on baking tray and keep warm in oven.

3 Working in batches, dip seafood and vegetables into batter and fry until golden and crisp, then transfer to oven. Lightly season with salt and serve with lemon wedges.

Baghdad eggs on simple flatbread

I created this as a breakfast special during the years I owned the all-day café Richmond Hill Café & Larder in the Melbourne suburb of Richmond. It is still a popular seller, I believe. The flatbread is also excellent alongside soup or a curry. If you have two small non-stick pans the ingredients for cooking the eggs can easily be doubled.

½ teaspoon cumin seeds
20 g butter
1 clove garlic, thinly sliced
1 tablespoon lemon juice
2 free-range eggs
sea salt and freshly ground
    black pepper
8 mint leaves, thinly sliced

SIMPLE FLATBREAD
125 g plain flour, plus extra
    for dusting
¼ teaspoon salt
2 teaspoons extra-virgin olive oil
⅓ cup (80 ml) tepid water

1 To make the flatbreads, put flour and salt into a food processor. With the motor running, trickle in olive oil and enough tepid water to make a dough (add gradually as you may not need it all), processing for 1–2 minutes until mixture forms a ball. Turn dough onto a workbench lightly dusted with flour and knead until smooth and silky. Put into a bowl and cover with a clean tea towel. Leave at room temperature for at least 30 minutes.

2 Preheat oven to 100°C and put a baking tray inside to warm.

3 Divide dough into 4 pieces each about the size of a small egg, then use a rolling pin to roll into flat rounds on a floured workbench.

4 Heat a dry cast-iron frying pan over high heat until very hot. Cook one dough round at a time for 2–3 minutes and then turn to cook the other side. (The cooked flatbread will have little burnt blisters on it.) Keep warm on the baking tray in the oven while cooking remaining flatbreads and eggs.

5 Dry-roast cumin seeds in a small frying pan over medium heat until fragrant, then grind with a mortar and pestle to a powder. Set aside.

6 Melt butter in a small non-stick frying pan over medium heat. When butter starts to foam, cook garlic for 30 seconds until it just starts to change colour. Add lemon juice and eggs and fry gently until set. Sprinkle over cumin. Serve on warm flatbread, seasoned with salt and pepper and sprinkled with mint.

Stephanie's twice-baked goat's cheese soufflés SERVES 6–8

These soufflés are not served in their dishes, so it is possible to use aluminium moulds or even teacups of about 150 ml capacity. To make blue cheese soufflés, substitute the same weight of creamy blue cheese for the goat's cheese.

80 g butter
60 g plain flour
350 ml milk, warmed
75 g fresh goat's cheese
1 tablespoon finely grated parmesan
2 tablespoons finely chopped flat-leaf parsley or flat-leaf parsley and other herbs
4 free-range eggs, separated
sea salt and freshly ground black pepper
2 cups (500 ml) pouring cream
green salad (optional), to serve

1 Preheat oven to 180°C. Melt 20 g of the butter and use to grease six to eight 150 ml-capacity soufflé dishes.

2 Melt remaining butter in a small heavy-based saucepan. Stir in flour and cook over medium heat, stirring, for 2 minutes. Gradually add milk, stirring all the while. Bring to a boil, then reduce heat and simmer for 5 minutes.

3 Mash goat's cheese until soft and add to hot sauce with parmesan and parsley (or parsley and other herbs). Allow to cool for a few minutes. Fold 3 egg yolks in thoroughly and taste for seasoning (save remaining yolk for another use). Beat egg whites until creamy, then fold quickly and lightly into cheese mixture. Divide mixture among prepared moulds and smooth surface of each. Stand moulds in a baking dish lined with a tea towel and pour in boiling water to come two-thirds up their sides. Bake for 20 minutes or until firm to the touch and well puffed. Remove soufflés from oven – they will deflate and look wrinkled. Allow to rest for 1–2 minutes, then gently ease out of moulds. Invert onto a plate covered with plastic film and leave to cool, then refrigerate until needed.

4 To serve, preheat oven to 180°C. Place soufflés upside down in a buttered ovenproof gratin dish, so that they are not touching. Pour over ⅓ cup (80 ml) cream per soufflé to moisten thoroughly. Return to oven for 15 minutes. The soufflés will look swollen and golden. Spoon any remaining cream from baking dish around to serve. Serve with a green salad, if desired.

Asparagus with coddled eggs

Egg coddlers can be made from patterned porcelain or toughened glass: whichever type you use, it must be watertight. Mostly they are made to hold just one egg, although I own glass ones that are intended to hold two. They are a lovely way to serve a special breakfast. Here the coddled eggs are used as a dipping sauce for asparagus spears. Choose the very best eggs.

80 g butter, melted, plus extra
    for greasing
6 large eggs (preferably newly laid
    free-range eggs)
sea salt and freshly ground
    black pepper
2 tablespoons freshly chopped
    flat-leaf parsley
1 tablespoon freshly chopped chervil
1 tablespoon freshly chopped chives
1 tablespoon freshly chopped
    French tarragon
1 cup (70 g) fine white breadcrumbs
24 asparagus spears of even size
¼ cup (60 ml) pouring cream, heated

1 Brush inside of 6 egg coddlers with 1 tablespoon of the melted butter. Break 1 or 2 eggs into each and lightly season. Mix herbs and divide among 6 small dishes (Chinese sauce dishes are an ideal size). Put remaining butter into a small saucepan with breadcrumbs. Over gentle heat, spoon crumbs over and over until they are a lovely toasted biscuit colour. Tip onto paper towel for a few minutes, then divide among another 6 small plates.

2 To coddle eggs, fill a saucepan large enough to take coddlers with water to a depth of 2–3 cm and bring to a simmer. Screw or clip on lids and put coddlers in pan. (The water should come two-thirds up sides of coddlers.) Cook for 4–5 minutes for a single egg, 6–7 minutes for 2.

3 Meanwhile, cook the asparagus in a saucepan of simmering salted water until just tender. Drain hot asparagus on a clean cloth. Roll asparagus in a buttered dish and divide among 6 serving plates. Remove coddlers from pan, carefully unscrew lids (they will be hot) and pour 2 teaspoons hot cream into each coddler; the eggs will continue to cook for 30 seconds or so. Arrange dishes of herbs and crumbs on each plate or on side plates. To enjoy this delicious dish, dip asparagus in egg, roll in herbs and crumbs – and bite!

The quality of the tomatoes, sherry vinegar and oil is what makes a splendid rather than an ordinary gazpacho. In late summer in Melbourne, a stall at my local farmers' market sells 'Grandpa' tomatoes – huge and meaty, they are ideal for this dish. I use a meat mincer for the vegetables, but a food processor will do. The texture should be coarse but there should not be large lumps.

1.5 kg ripe tomatoes, chopped
200 g Lebanese or long cucumber,
**   peeled and chopped**
150 g red capsicum (pepper), chopped
2 cloves garlic, peeled
100 g crustless sourdough bread
2 cups (500 ml) cold water, plus
**   extra if needed**
3 teaspoons salt
freshly ground black pepper
**   or Tabasco**
½ cup (125 ml) sherry vinegar
½ cup (125 ml) extra-virgin olive oil

1 Mince or process vegetables, garlic and bread and transfer to a large bowl. Stir in water, salt, pepper or Tabasco and vinegar. Refrigerate for at least 1 hour (even overnight) for bread to swell and flavours to blend.

2 Just before serving, stir in olive oil and taste for seasoning, then season with salt and pepper. The soup should have quite a tang to it. It may need extra water, too, depending on the bread and tomatoes used.

Minestrone with fresh borlotti beans and cavolo nero SERVES 8

Cavolo nero, or Tuscan kale as it is also known, is a particularly delicious member of the kale family. The leaves do not disintegrate easily and, when shredded into ribbons, add drama and flavour to this classic dish, of which there must be thousands of interpretations. The central rib of each leaf needs to be removed and discarded as it will never soften. Any soup left over can be reheated the next day, when it can be called *ribollita*, meaning reboiled. If you cannot obtain fresh borlotti beans, use 200 g dried beans, soaked overnight, drained and precooked, or 2½ cups (375 g) precooked frozen borlotti beans.

½ cup (125 ml) olive oil
20 g butter
3 onions, finely chopped
3 cloves garlic, finely chopped
2 carrots, diced
2 sticks celery, diced
1 × 200 g piece pork rind, cut into
    3 (optional)
1 kg fresh borlotti beans, shelled
    to yield 2¾ cups (about 400 g)
rind from a piece of parmesan
1 bay leaf
1 cup (250 ml) tomato passata or
    4 ripe tomatoes, peeled, seeded
    and finely chopped
1.5 litres Chicken Stock, Veal Stock
    (see page 134), beef stock or water
100 g shredded cavolo nero or Savoy cabbage
3 zucchini (courgettes), diced
125 g green beans, chopped
sea salt and freshly ground black pepper
extra-virgin olive oil, for drizzling
freshly grated parmesan, to serve

1 Heat olive oil and butter in a stockpot until butter is foaming, then add onion and garlic. Cook gently over low heat until onion has softened. Add carrot, celery and pork rind (if using) and cook gently, turning to coat vegetables. After 5 minutes add borlotti beans, parmesan rind, bay leaf, tomato passata or chopped tomato and stock.

2 Cover and simmer for 1½ hours. Add cavolo nero or cabbage, zucchini and green beans and simmer for 30 minutes. Taste for seasoning and discard cheese and pork rinds. Serve in wide soup bowls, drizzled with olive oil. Offer parmesan at the table.

Jerusalem artichoke soup

Despite their name, Jerusalem artichokes do not come from Jerusalem, nor are they related to globe artichokes. They are a root vegetable related to sunflowers. By following the same method using other vegetables other lovely soups can be made: invent your own combination.

juice of 1 lemon
750 g Jerusalem artichokes
2 potatoes
80 g butter
1 large onion, halved lengthways and
thinly sliced
2 cloves garlic, sliced
2 sticks celery, sliced
1.5 litres Chicken Stock (page 134)
sea salt and freshly ground
black pepper
15 chives, finely chopped
⅓ cup (80 ml) pouring cream or
sour cream
Garlic Croûtons (see page 140),
to serve

1 Fill a large bowl with water and add lemon juice. Peel Jerusalem artichokes, cut into walnut-sized chunks, then drop into bowl of acidulated (lemon) water. Peel potatoes, cut into chunks, then drop into bowl of acidulated water.

2 Drain artichoke and potato, then tip onto a tea towel and dry well.

3 Melt butter in a large saucepan over high heat. When butter foams, add onion, garlic and celery. Stir to coat vegetables in melted butter. Add drained artichoke and potato and stir for 1–2 minutes. Pour chicken stock into the pan and bring to a simmer. Reduce heat to low and simmer for 10 minutes or until all vegetables are tender when pierced with a fine skewer.

4 Transfer soup in batches to a blender (or food processor) and cover blender lid with a thick dry tea towel; hot liquids can force up the lid, spraying hot liquid that can burn. Carefully blend until smooth. Tip soup through a coarse strainer into a bowl. Use a spatula or wooden spoon to push soup through strainer and break up any lumps. Repeat with remaining soup. Return soup to cleaned pan.

5 Reheat soup over low–medium heat until it reaches simmering point, stirring in a little water or stock if the soup is too thick. Season to taste with salt and pepper. Ladle soup into bowls, sprinkle with chives, then swirl in a dollop of cream or sour cream and top with croûtons. Serve with extra croûtons offered alongside.

Pumpkin, coconut and seafood soup

This is a very speedily made soup. By separately poaching or steaming a generous piece of chunky fish or pan-searing some fat scallops (or both), this soup can become a one-dish dinner.

**400 g peeled and seeded pumpkin,
    cut into 1 cm-thick slices**
1 tablespoon vegetable oil
1 onion, finely chopped
4 cloves garlic, finely chopped
**1 fresh long green or red chilli,
    seeded and chopped**
**2 teaspoons shrimp paste (see page 140),
    or to taste**
3 cups (750 ml) water
2 teaspoons fish sauce, or to taste
200 ml coconut milk
sea salt
**8 scallops and/or 1 × 400 g thick fillet
    of white fish, such as barramundi,
    hapuka or blue eye trevalla, cut into
    bite-sized pieces**
**1 × 2 cm-long piece ginger, very finely
    chopped or grated**
**¼ cup (3 tablespoons) roughly
    chopped coriander**

1 Half-fill a wok with water and bring to a boil. Put pumpkin into a bamboo steamer over the wok, then cover and steam for 10 minutes or until tender.

2 Heat oil in an enamelled cast-iron casserole over medium heat and sauté onion, garlic and chilli for 8–10 minutes or until onion is well softened. Stir in shrimp paste, then add pumpkin, water and fish sauce. Bring to a simmer and simmer for 3 minutes.

3 Transfer soup in batches to a blender (or food processor) and cover blender lid with a thick dry tea towel; hot liquids can force up the lid, spraying hot liquid that can burn. Carefully blend until smooth. Tip each batch into a bowl. Continue until all soup is smoothly blended. Rinse out saucepan and return soup to the pan. Add coconut milk. Bring to a simmer over medium heat and taste for salt and pungency, then adjust with more fish sauce or salt if desired. Set aside.

4 Sear scallops in a non-stick frying pan over high heat for 1 minute on each side. If using fish, half-fill wok with water and bring to boil. Put fish into a bamboo steamer over the wok and steam for 5–8 minutes or until cooked through.

5 Reheat soup and stir in ginger and coriander. Transfer scallops and/or fish to hot soup. Ladle into warmed soup bowls and serve at once.

Watercress, sorrel and potato soup

This recipe calls for more watercress than sorrel, but if you happen to have more sorrel than watercress on hand, just reverse the proportions and the results will be fine. To remove the sorrel leaves from the stems, bend each sorrel leaf in half and pull the stem up and along the leaf (a bit like pulling up a zipper). The stem end and the central stem will come away, leaving you with two pieces of leaf. While the mustard cress butter is optional, it makes a lovely addition.

30 g unsalted butter (or even better, use the Mustard Cress Butter below)
2 spring onions, trimmed and sliced
2 cloves garlic, finely chopped
450 g waxy potatoes, cut into 2 cm cubes
1 bay leaf
1 litre water
65 g picked watercress leaves and tender stems, well washed and dried
60 g sorrel leaves, well washed, dried and stems removed
sea salt and freshly ground black pepper
cress sprigs (optional), to serve

MUSTARD CRESS BUTTER

60 g unsalted butter, softened
a few drops lemon juice
¼ cup (3 tablespoons) snipped mustard cress, roughly chopped
sea salt and freshly ground black pepper

1 To make the mustard cress butter, if using, combine all ingredients in a food processor or work them all together in a bowl using a fork. Scrape butter onto a piece of baking paper and form a roll. (Wrap in a doubled piece of foil and refrigerate for a day or so or freeze for up to 3 months.)

2 Melt butter in a large saucepan over medium heat and sauté spring onion and garlic for 2 minutes. Add potato and bay leaf and turn to sweat potato in butter. Add water, bring to a simmer over medium heat, then cover and cook gently over low heat for 15 minutes or until potato is tender. Drop in watercress and sorrel and simmer for 2 minutes. Remove bay leaf.

3 Transfer soup in batches to a blender (or food processor) and cover blender lid with a thick dry tea towel; hot liquids can force up the lid, spraying hot liquid that can burn. Carefully blend until smooth. (For a lovely baby purée-smooth soup, press each batch through a coarse-meshed stainless-steel sieve into a clean, large saucepan.) Taste for salt and pepper and season as required. Reheat gently to serve. Top each serve with a slice of mustard cress butter, if using, and sprig of cress, if desired.

Warm sauté of zucchini, pine nuts and currants

The combination of pine nuts and currants is frequently encountered in Sicilian-inspired dishes. This dish is speedy to prepare and cook, and is at its best immediately after cooking, when the pine nuts are warm and the zucchini still a little crisp.

2 tablespoons currants
2 tablespoons red-wine vinegar
2 tablespoons extra-virgin olive oil
¼ cup (40 g) pine nuts
400 g zucchini (courgettes), cut lengthways
    into 5 mm-thick slices
1 clove garlic, finely chopped
2 teaspoons lemon juice
12 mint leaves, finely shredded
sea salt and freshly ground black pepper
sprig mint (optional), to serve

1 Preheat oven to 100°C and put an ovenproof serving dish inside to keep warm.

2 Soak currants in vinegar for 10 minutes, then set aside.

3 Heat 2 teaspoons of the olive oil in a frying pan over medium heat and fry pine nuts for 2 minutes or until golden, then tip onto a paper towel-lined plate and set aside.

4 Heat remaining olive oil in a large non-stick frying pan over high heat and add zucchini slices in a single layer (remember to carefully place them in the hot oil, not drop them). Don't shake the pan. The aim is for each slice to colour evenly and quickly. Turn slices carefully and cook until well coloured but still crisp, then transfer to serving dish in oven. Wipe out pan with paper towel and place over high heat.

5 Add garlic to pan and cook for a few seconds, then add currant/vinegar mixture; the vinegar will hiss, splutter and reduce almost instantly. Add pine nuts to the pan, shaking to mix with currant mixture, then spoon over zucchini. Add lemon juice and mint, then season with salt and pepper and top with a mint sprig, if using. Serve at once.

Sweet-and-sour pumpkin with mint

Use a dry-fleshed pumpkin such as a Queensland blue or a green-and-yellow-splashed kent (jap) for this dish to make sure the slices don't break up when sautéing. The texture of the pumpkin is best if eaten within a few hours of cooking. If intended as part of an antipasti platter, don't refrigerate it. If it is to be used to top a pizza, then the finished pumpkin can be stored, covered, in the refrigerator for a couple of days. This recipe is based on one in the excellent book *Verdura: Vegetables Italian Style* by Viana La Place, a treasure-house of marvellous vegetable dishes.

2 tablespoons extra-virgin olive oil
2 cloves garlic, unpeeled and bruised
250 g peeled and seeded pumpkin,
    cut into 5 mm-thick slices
1 tablespoon caster sugar
2 tablespoons red-wine vinegar
sea salt and freshly ground black pepper
12 mint leaves, torn or roughly chopped
grissini (optional), to serve

1 Heat olive oil in a large non-stick frying pan over low heat and sauté garlic cloves for 5 minutes or until golden. Discard garlic. Carefully arrange pumpkin in a single layer in the pan. Increase heat to low–medium and cook for 2–3 minutes. Turn pumpkin carefully and cook for a further 2–3 minutes; the slices should be well coloured and cooked through when inserted with a skewer. Place pumpkin in a layer on a plate.

2 Discard any oil in the pan, then place over high heat. Tip in sugar and vinegar, then swirl to dissolve sugar and slightly reduce vinegar. Spoon vinegar syrup over pumpkin slices and season with salt and pepper. Scatter with mint.

3 Leave at room temperature for at least 1 hour before eating. Serve with grissini, if desired.

Barley and mushroom risotto

The cooking method is the same as for a classic risotto, but even though the barley has been 'pearled' it still takes longer to cook than rice. Barley will always retain a slight chewiness in the grain and it has a delightfully nutty flavour.

1 cup (250 ml) hot water
15 g dried porcini mushrooms
2 cups (500 ml) Chicken Stock (see page 134)
40 g butter
1 tablespoon extra-virgin olive oil
½ onion, finely chopped
2 cloves garlic, finely chopped
1 cup (200 g) pearl barley (see page 140)
¼ cup (60 ml) vino cotto (see page 140)
    or red-wine vinegar
100 g button mushrooms, trimmed and sliced
sea salt and freshly ground black pepper
¼ cup (3 tablespoons) chopped flat-leaf parsley

1 Pour the boiling water over porcini and soak for 10 minutes. Lift porcini onto a chopping board and strain liquid through a fine-meshed sieve into a small saucepan. Add stock to saucepan and heat over low heat until hot. Roughly chop porcini.

2 Melt 20 g of the butter with the olive oil in another small saucepan or wide-based pan over high heat, then cook onion and garlic for 1 minute, stirring. Add chopped porcini and barley and stir well for 1 minute or until each grain is shiny with oil and butter. Add vino cotto or vinegar and let it sizzle and evaporate.

3 Reduce heat to medium, then start adding hot stock one ladleful at a time. Stir after each addition. A barley risotto will take 30 minutes to cook so be patient. After half of the stock has been added (after perhaps 15 minutes), add sliced mushrooms. Leave them to soften for 1–2 minutes before stirring them through barley. Continue adding remaining stock, a ladleful at a time, until all stock is used and the barley is tender. Season with salt and pepper, then stir in parsley and remaining butter. Turn off heat and leave, covered, for 3 minutes or so before serving.

Spring ragoût of artichoke hearts, turnips, broad beans and peas

This exquisite first course is a labour of love as not only does it feature double-peeled broad beans, peeled baby turnips and artichokes trimmed to the heart, but also properly prepared shelled peas straight from the bushes. This delicious dish could also be served alongside grilled or sautéed chicken breasts or escalopes of veal or with grilled wood-fired bread for sopping up the pan juices.

8 cloves garlic
1 kg broad beans in pods, shelled
ice cubes
60 g unsalted butter, chopped
4 Trimmed and Cooked Artichoke Hearts
     (see page 135), halved or quartered,
     depending on size
12 baby turnips, peeled
1 cup (250 ml) Chicken Stock (see page 134)
500 g peas in pods, shelled (to yield 160 g
     shelled peas)
2 teaspoons roughly chopped French tarragon
1 tablespoon finely chopped flat-leaf parsley
freshly ground black pepper
grilled wood-fired bread (optional), to serve

1 Put garlic into a saucepan and cover with water. Bring slowly to the boil over low–medium heat, then drain. Repeat, then peel and set aside in a bowl.

2 Cook broad beans in a pan of boiling water for 1 minute only. Immediately drain and tip into a bowl of iced cold water. Enlist help and double-peel broad beans. Reserve until needed.

3 Melt 30 g of the butter in a sauté pan over medium heat. Once it starts to froth add artichoke pieces, turnips and peeled garlic and sauté until artichoke pieces become golden flecked with brown. Add chicken stock and peas, then cook, covered, for 5 minutes.

4 Uncover, scatter over broad beans and herbs and shake gently to mix; there should be very little liquid remaining in the pan. If it still looks sloppy increase heat to high and continue to shake the pan. Add remaining butter to melt and form a small amount of sauce. Taste for seasoning; there probably won't be any need to add salt. Grind over pepper and serve at once, with grilled bread, if desired.

Diana's bread-and-butter pickled cucumbers

My sister Diana has always had great success with growing cucumbers. Her version of this well-known pickle is delightful. Not only is it great served with cold cuts, it also makes a wonderful addition to a good-quality cheddar sandwich.

500 ml freshly picked young cucumbers, unpeeled (the crunchier the better)
1 onion (about 200 g), very thinly sliced
1½ tablespoons kitchen salt
¼ cup (60 ml) hot water

PICKLING LIQUID
1 cup (250 ml) white vinegar
1 cup (220 g) white sugar
2 teaspoons mustard seeds
1 teaspoon chopped dill
¼ teaspoon ground turmeric
¼ teaspoon chilli flakes

1 Slice cucumbers very thinly in a food processor using the slicing attachment or with a plastic vegetable slicer (this is more accurate, but more dangerous than a food processor). Mix cucumber and onion in a mixing bowl. Dissolve salt in hot water in a stainless-steel saucepan over medium heat, stirring with a wooden spoon until completely dissolved, then pour over cucumber mixture. Mix through and leave for 3 hours. Rinse saucepan.

2 Tip cucumber and onion into a colander resting over a plate or bowl. Press with the back of a large metal spoon to extract as much liquid as possible.

3 To make the pickling liquid, mix all ingredients in the rinsed-out saucepan. Bring to a simmer over medium heat, stirring until sugar has dissolved. Tip cucumber and onion into pickling liquid and simmer for 2–3 minutes, stirring once or twice. Remove from heat and leave to cool in the saucepan, then spoon or ladle into sterilised jars (see page 140), ensuring the cucumber mixture is covered with pickling liquid. Seal, label and date the jars. (Store unopened jars in a cool, dark place for up to a year. Once opened, store in the refrigerator.)

Mains

Pappardelle with peas, lettuce and prosciutto

This delicate and gentle sauce is perfect with tender homemade pasta. The instructions may at first look long and off-putting, but with two or three people working together this amount of pasta can be made from scratch in less than 15 minutes (excluding the one-hour resting time). While I like to hand-cut pappardelle, you could just run the dough through the pasta machine cutters if you prefer.

salt
40 g unsalted butter
2 tablespoons extra-virgin olive oil
6 slices prosciutto, cut widthways into
    1 cm-wide strips
12 cos lettuce leaves, hard stalks
    cut away, leaves cut widthways
    into 3 cm-wide strips
2 cloves garlic, thinly sliced
500 g peas in pod (to yield
    160 g shelled peas)
1 cup (250 ml) pouring cream
2 tablespoons chopped flat-leaf parsley
sea salt and freshly ground black pepper
grated parmesan, to serve

FRESH PASTA
2 cups (300 g) plain flour, plus extra
    for dusting
3 free-range eggs, lightly beaten
1 free-range egg yolk (if needed)

1 To make the pasta, put flour into a food processor. With motor running, add eggs. Process for a few minutes until dough clings together and feels springy (it should not feel sticky); if mixture is too dry, add extra egg yolk. Tip dough onto a floured workbench, knead for a few minutes, then wrap in plastic film and rest for 1 hour at room temperature.

2 Clear a large space on your workbench and have a bowl of plain flour nearby. All surfaces must be dry. If serving pasta immediately, bring a large saucepan or pasta pot of lightly salted water to the boil. Divide dough in half. Press each half into a rectangle about 8 cm wide. Pass this piece of dough through pasta machine rollers set to its thickest setting. If dough comes through ragged at the edges, fold it in 3, then turn it 90 degrees and roll it through twice more. Change to next-thickest setting and pass the dough through 3–4 times. Continue in this manner until dough has passed through thinnest setting desired. If dough gets too long to handle comfortably, cut it into 2–3 pieces and roll each piece separately.

3 Either cut pasta sheets into 10–15 mm-wide pappardelle, or run them over cutting rollers. Lay cut pasta on flour-dusted bench or a clean tea towel and roll and cut remaining dough. Use as soon as possible, or hang over a length of dowelling (or a broom handle) or the back of a chair to dry. It will take 10 minutes or so for pasta to dry in a well-ventilated room.

4 Heat butter and olive oil in a large non-stick frying pan or sauté pan over low heat and gently sauté prosciutto until the fat starts to run. Add lettuce and garlic, then cover pan and cook gently over low heat for 5 minutes or until lettuce is limp.

5 Meanwhile, cook pappardelle in a pan of lightly salted boiling water. It will take just a couple of minutes to be correctly al dente. Drain pasta, then return it to hot empty pasta pot while you finish the sauce.

6 Add peas and cream to prosciutto mixture, cover and cook for 5 minutes or until tender. Uncover pan and increase heat to medium, then cook for 2–3 minutes or until cream starts to thicken and deepen in colour. Toss in pasta and parsley, then season with salt and pepper. Mix well and tip into a warmed serving dish and serve. Offer grated parmesan.

Spinach and ricotta pasta 'roly-poly'

This dish is good for a party. Although it seems to involve many stages, the final baking is very simple and it can be served with a lot less anxiety than is the case when cooking and dividing up pasta for a crowd.

500 g spinach leaves (to yield 250 g after stemming), washed well
salt
2 tablespoons extra-virgin olive oil
1 onion, finely chopped
100 g sliced pancetta, 6 slices reserved and the rest finely chopped
3 cloves garlic, finely chopped
500 g fresh ricotta
150 g blue cheese of choice, crumbled
100 g parmesan, grated
½ teaspoon freshly grated nutmeg
sea salt and freshly ground black pepper
300 g Fresh Pasta (see page 50)
20 g butter, for greasing
200 ml pouring cream
8–10 sage leaves

1 Cook spinach, covered, in a large saucepan of lightly salted boiling over medium heat, stirring once, for 4 minutes or until collapsed. Drain. Run under cold water, then drain again and press with a saucepan lid or back of a saucer. Roll in a dry tea towel and twist ends in opposite directions to extract as much liquid as possible. Pulse-chop in a food processor for a few seconds.

2 Heat olive oil in a large non-stick frying pan over medium heat. Sauté onion and chopped pancetta for 8–10 minutes, stirring until onion has softened well and pancetta started to colour. Add garlic and sauté for 30 seconds, then stir in spinach. Stir well and cook for 1–2 minutes to evaporate moisture. Spread out on a tray and leave to cool.

3 Combine ricotta, blue cheese and two-thirds of the parmesan in a bowl. Add nutmeg and season with salt and pepper. Using clean hands, mix spinach mixture with cheese mixture, squeezing and pressing to mix really well. Season with salt and pepper.

4 Roll pasta sheets using a pasta machine, moving through each setting until the second last notch, then cut into 5 even pieces about 20 cm long. Bring a pasta pot or large heavy-based saucepan of well salted water to the boil over high heat. Have a large bowl of cold water and 2 dry tea towels spread out on a workbench alongside the stove. Drop 3 pasta sheets at a time into simmering water and cook for 3 minutes. Carefully lift out each cooked sheet and drop into cold water. Lift each sheet from cold water and spread out on a dry tea towel; don't overlap as they will stick and tear.

5 Preheat oven to 180°C. Butter a 30 cm × 22 cm baking dish.

6 Lay 2 sheets of pasta side by side in buttered dish and overlapping down centre of dish by 2–3 cm; pasta sheets will come up sides of baking dish. Lay 1 pasta sheet down the centre of the baking dish. Put half of the filling down the centre and flatten it into a squared-off 'log' of filling. Cover filling with another pasta sheet. Spread remaining filling over pasta sheet. Fold overhanging pasta sheets over second layer of filling. Place an extra pasta sheet over the top and tuck it down the sides of the roll. If the 'roly-poly' fits a little too snugly in the baking dish, then curve it a little to fit. Brush top and sides of pasta with cream. Drape over reserved pancetta. Place sage leaves down length of 'roly-poly'. Scatter with remaining parmesan and drizzle remaining cream over and around.

7 Cover baking dish with foil and bake for 20 minutes. Remove foil and bake for a further 10 minutes. Leave 'roly-poly' to cool and settle for a few minutes before slicing and serving.

Pasta with sardines and fennel

This is a Sicilian treat - sardines and fennel in one recipe! These powerful flavours are combined with smooth pasta, sweet currants and irresistible pine nuts. Sometimes this dish appears with spaghetti, sometimes with a hollow pasta such as rigatoni or bucatini, and I have also seen it layered between pasta sheets and baked as for a lasagne – an idea that is definitely worth trying.

⅓ cup (50 g) currants
½ cup (125 ml) dry white wine or water
½ teaspoon saffron stamens
2 tablespoons warm water
100 ml extra-virgin olive oil, plus extra
 if needed
1 clove garlic, bruised
60 g fresh breadcrumbs
2 outer fennel layers, cut in half
salt
500 g dried pasta
1 onion, finely chopped
1 cup very finely chopped fennel fronds
 (including some of the inner layers
 of fennel bulb)
1 teaspoon chilli flakes
½ cup (80 g) pine nuts
12 fresh sardines, filleted
sea salt and freshly ground black pepper

1 Preheat oven to 100°C and put 4 ovenproof pasta bowls inside to warm.

2 Soak currants in wine or water in a small bowl for 30 minutes. Soak saffron in warm water in another small bowl until needed.

3 Heat 2 tablespoons of the olive oil and bruised garlic in a large non-stick frying pan over medium heat, then stir in breadcrumbs. Stir until crumbs are golden and feel a bit sandy. Tip breadcrumbs into a bowl and set aside; discard garlic. Wipe out pan with paper towel.

4 Add fennel to a large saucepan or pasta pot of lightly salted water and bring to the boil (this flavours the cooking water). Add pasta and cook until al dente. (Be guided by the instructions on the packet, but check several minutes earlier than indicated.)

5 Meanwhile, heat remaining olive oil in a heavy-based frying pan over medium heat and sauté onion and half of the fennel fronds for 6–8 minutes or until well softened. Add currants and any liquid, chilli flakes, saffron and its soaking water and pine nuts and stir to mix. Add sardines, increase heat to high and stir for 1–2 minutes until just cooked. Remove pan from heat.

6 Drain cooked pasta and shake well, discarding fennel. Return pasta immediately to the hot pan. Tip in sardine/fennel sauce and shake and stir to mix; don't worry if sardines have broken up. Add salt and pepper if necessary. If the pasta looks at all dry, add an extra drizzle of olive oil. Scatter with remaining fennel fronds.

7 Divide pasta mixture among warm pasta bowls and sprinkle with breadcrumbs, then serve.

Tarragon roast chicken for Holly and Lisa

My daughters love roast chicken and this recipe is very often the first choice when we get together around the table. A special treat in summer would be to serve this with freshly picked green beans. You could also roast a selection of seasonal vegetables, or French shallots or small onions in the pan at the same time, as I did when this was photographed.

1 × 1.8 kg free-range chicken
sea salt and freshly ground black pepper
3 good-sized sprigs French tarragon
1 thick slice lemon
1 clove garlic, unpeeled and bruised
60 g butter, chopped and softened
1 tablespoon extra-virgin olive oil
1 cup (250 ml) dry white wine
1 tablespoon pouring cream

1 Place unwrapped chicken breast-side up and uncovered on a plate in the refrigerator to allow skin to dry out for at least 1 hour.

2 Preheat oven to 220°C.

3 Wipe chicken inside and out with paper towel. Remove giblets and neck, if present, and reserve them for making stock for another dish. Season chicken inside and out with salt and pepper. Place tarragon, lemon and garlic inside cavity. Rub 30 g of the soft butter all over breast and legs and put rest inside cavity. Truss chicken with kitchen string if you wish (I usually don't).

4 Brush a roasting pan with olive oil and place chicken in it on its side. Roast for 20 minutes. Carefully turn chicken to the other side, trying not to tear skin, and roast for a further 20 minutes. Reduce oven temperature to 180°C and turn the chicken breast-side up. Baste with pan juices and roast for a further 20 minutes or until cooked through.

5 Remove roasting pan from oven and tip bird so that juices, herbs, lemon and garlic inside cavity fall into pan. Place chicken on a warmed ovenproof dish and keep warm while you make a simple sauce. Tip away fat and place pan over high heat. Press garlic, lemon and tarragon with a wooden spoon and cook for 1 minute, stirring and scraping with the wooden spoon. Stir in wine. When bubbling strongly, stir in cream. Strain sauce into a warm jug.

6 Joint the chicken to make self-service easier. Remove legs and wings, and cut the breast meat into chunks (I use strong kitchen scissors to do this). Pour over sauce, or offer it separately.

Stephanie's chicken provençale

I believe that a casserole of chicken is best eaten as soon as it is ready. I do not enjoy reheated chicken casseroles very much – the pieces seem to lose their plumpness and succulence and are very quickly transformed into rags.

1 × 1.8 kg free-range chicken
sea salt and freshly ground
**   black pepper**
2 red capsicums (peppers), halved
2 yellow capsicums (peppers), halved
2 anchovy fillets, chopped
2 tablespoons very freshly chopped
**   flat-leaf parsley**
18 large black olives, pitted and halved
2 tablespoons olive oil
1 onion, sliced into rings
4 cloves garlic, finely chopped
½ cup (125 ml) dry white wine or
**   half wine, half vermouth**
4 large ripe tomatoes, peeled or
**   1 × 410 g tin peeled tomatoes,**
**   roughly chopped**
1 bay leaf
1 large sprig thyme
4 small zucchini (courgette),
**   cut into chunks**
green salad and boiled small unpeeled
**   waxy potatoes, to serve**

1 Joint chicken into thighs, drumsticks and wings and cut each breast fillet in half, keeping it on the bone. You should have 10 pieces. Season.

2 Grill capsicums, skin-side up, until black. Wrap in a cloth or enclose in a plastic bag for 10 minutes, then remove skin, cores and seeds. Slice thickly and set aside. Put anchovies into a bowl and stand bowl over simmering water to melt anchovies. Stir in parsley and olives and set aside.

3 Preheat oven to 200°C. Select a large, enamelled cast-iron casserole that will hold the chicken and vegetables and can be used both for the initial browning and the completed dish. Heat olive oil and brown chicken in batches, so that the heat remains high and there is a good sizzle. Transfer browned pieces to a plate. Pour off most of the fat and lightly sauté onion for 5 minutes. Add garlic and replace chicken, with drumsticks and thighs on the bottom. Add any juices that have collected on the plate. Reheat until there is a sizzle from the casserole. Pour over wine and allow to sizzle up the sides and quickly reduce. Add tomato and any juice, plus bay leaf and thyme. Cover with foil and a lid and bake in oven for 45 minutes.

4 Stir casserole gently and add sliced capsicums and zucchini. Replace lid and cook for a further 20 minutes. The chicken should be tender but not collapsed and the zucchini should still be a little firm.

5 When ready to serve, rebubble, uncovered, on top of stove and scatter with the parsley, olive and anchovy mixture. Serve with a green salad and small waxy potatoes boiled in their skins.

Chicken and leek pie

I think everybody loves a pie, especially one with generous chunks of filling in a savoury sauce. This pie makes great picnic food if completely enclosed in pastry (rather than having only a pastry lid), as the filling sets quite firmly. To make individual pies, centre some cold filling on a 16 cm square of puff pastry, then pull up each corner to meet its opposite corner and seal the edges. Repeat until you have desired number of pies. Brush with eggwash and bake at 200°C for 25 minutes.

**1.2 kg boned free-range chicken thighs,
    skin removed**
sea salt and freshly ground black pepper
2 tablespoons plain flour
**2 large leeks, quartered lengthways
    and sliced**
100 g unsalted butter
**½ cup (6 tablespoons) freshly chopped
    flat-leaf parsley**
⅔ cup (160 ml) milk
1 cup (250 ml) pouring cream
1 free-range egg
puff pastry or mashed potato, to serve

1 Chop each chicken thigh into 12 bite-sized pieces and toss with seasoned flour (easiest done in a plastic bag). Wash leek well and dry in a cloth. Melt half the butter in a large frying pan or enamelled casserole and sauté leek for 10 minutes over medium heat until well softened. Tip into a bowl.

2 Melt half the remaining butter in same pan and sauté half the chicken pieces until golden and barely cooked. Transfer to bowl with leek. Repeat with remainder of butter and chicken. Toss chicken with leek and add parsley. Return half the mixture to the pan, add half the milk and half the cream and allow to bubble for about 5 minutes. Transfer to a clean bowl and repeat with remainder of chicken mixture, milk and cream. Combine both batches and check seasoning. Cool.

3 Preheat oven to 200°C.

4 Mix egg with a pinch of salt to make eggwash. Pack chicken filling into a deep 1.5 litre-capacity pie dish and cover with puff pastry or pipe on mashed potato to make a crust.

5 Brush with eggwash and bake for 25–30 minutes until golden and filling is bubbling around edges. Warn diners to wait a few minutes before they tuck in, as the pie will be piping hot.

Barbecued quail with myrtle

Quail has a delicate flavour that is complemented by many other ingredients, and it cooks very quickly. It is mandatory to lick your fingers! It can get a bit messy, so it might be a good idea to offer damp cotton towels at the end of eating this. (If myrtle sprigs are not available, then sprigs of rosemary or fresh bay leaves could be substituted.)

4 quails
⅓ cup (80 ml) extra-virgin olive oil,
    plus extra for drizzling
2½ tablespoons vino cotto
    (see page 140)
8 × 10 cm-long myrtle sprigs
    (with or without berries)
freshly ground black pepper
sea salt

1 Using kitchen scissors, cut up the back of each quail along either side of the backbone right through to the neck opening. Pull out backbone. Open out each bird and remove the heart and liver (if present). Rinse bird quickly under cold water and then pat really dry with paper towel. Turn each quail skin-side up and press firmly on the breastbone to flatten it with your hand. Repeat with all the quail. (This is called 'spatchcocking' or 'butterflying'.)

2 Mix olive oil and 2 tablespoons of vino cotto in a baking dish. Roughly squash any berries on myrtle sprigs into the mixture. Grind in a good amount of black pepper and drop in myrtle sprigs. Add quail and turn over and over for 1 minute or so, then leave to marinate, flesh-side down, for up to 1 hour (any longer and you will have to refrigerate).

3 If using a charcoal fire, ensure coals are white-hot. Otherwise, heat a char-grill pan or barbecue grill-plate until hot. Lift quails from marinade, letting any extra marinade drip back into the baking dish; hopefully the myrtle sprigs will be sticking to the birds at this stage.

4 (If using a hinged metal grill, arrange the quails evenly on one side and close the hinge firmly.) Cook flesh-side facing heat for about 6 minutes. Turn carefully and crisp skin-side for 2 minutes. Turn back to the other side if you are concerned that they are not sufficiently cooked for your taste. (Quail is especially delicious if cooked so that the breast meat is still faintly pink.) The myrtle sprigs should be nicely charred.

5 Transfer quails to a warm platter and drizzle with remaining vino cotto and 2 teaspoons extra olive oil. Leave to rest, skin-side down, for 5 minutes before serving. Sprinkle with salt before eating.

Classic corned beef

The term 'corned' is an old one referring to the curing of beef with grains of salt, once called corns of salt. As most corned meat these days is only mildly salted, it is hard to pass up a mustard sauce made from the cooking broth. And as corned beef and mustard sandwiches (with or without pickled cucumbers) are so fabulous, it is always a good idea to cook a big chunk of meat. Hot 'salt beef on rye' sandwiches, accompanied by bowls of dill pickles are a classic item in several of New York's famous delis.

1.5 kg corned or pickled silverside
    or girello
6 cloves
2 onions, unpeeled
7 carrots
1 stick celery, roughly chopped
1 teaspoon black peppercorns
2 bay leaves
12 pickling onions, peeled but
    root end left on
12 potatoes
knob of butter
freshly chopped flat-leaf parsley
1 quantity Sauce Ravigote
    (see page 136)

MUSTARD SAUCE

3 cups (750 ml) corned beef
    cooking broth
40 g butter
2 tablespoons plain flour
1 tablespoon dry mustard
2 tablespoons finely chopped
    flat-leaf parsley
2 tablespoons pouring cream
juice of ½ lemon
sea salt and freshly ground
    black pepper

1 Select a deep enamelled cast-iron casserole with room for both meat and vegetables. Put meat into pot and cover with cold water. Bring to a boil, then drain. Return meat to rinsed-out pot. Push 3 cloves into each onion and chop 3 of the carrots. Add onions, chopped carrot, celery, peppercorns and bay leaves to pot. Barely cover with water and bring to a boil, then adjust heat to a steady simmer and cook for about 2 hours (40 minutes per 500 g) with lid slightly ajar.

2 Transfer meat to a dish and strain broth, reserving 3 cups (750 ml) for making the sauce. Discard vegetables. Return meat and broth to rinsed-out pot and add pickling onions and remaining carrots, cut into thirds. Simmer for 30 minutes or until both meat and vegetables are tender.

3 Meanwhile, preheat oven to 100°C. Cook potatoes in boiling salted water until tender, then drain and toss with butter and parsley. Transfer to a dish and keep warm in oven. Remove meat and garnishing vegetables to a hot platter. Wrap platter in a double sheet of foil and keep warm in oven while you make the sauces.

4 To make the mustard sauce, boil broth in a saucepan rapidly until reduced by one-third. Melt butter in another saucepan and, when foaming, stir in flour and dry mustard. Cook for 2–3 minutes, stirring, then gradually whisk in hot reduced broth until smooth and boiling. Add parsley, cream and lemon juice. taste and adjust seasoning, then transfer sauce to a hot jug.

5 To serve, slice meat thickly, then moisten with a few spoonfuls of broth and surround with onions, carrot and potatoes. Serve with mustard sauce and a bowl of sauce ravigote.

Simplest beef stew

This stew is a good example of how you can fling everything together in 15 minutes and forget about it while it's cooking. Experiment with ingredients: you may want to include caraway seeds or chilli paste or chutney, for example. Ensure that the paprika you use is of top quality – my favourite is Spanish, sold in a small square tin. It makes all the difference to the flavour of the dish.

1.5 kg chuck or blade steak,
   cut into large cubes
60 g plain flour
2 teaspoons best-quality paprika
1 × 400 g tin peeled tomatoes in juice
1 cup (250 ml) white or red wine
2 onions, diced
2 cloves garlic, sliced
1 stick celery, thinly sliced
3 carrots, cut into chunks
3 potatoes, cut into chunks
sea salt and freshly ground black pepper
natural yoghurt (optional) and pickled
   dill cucumbers (optional), to serve

1 Preheat oven to 180°C.

2 Roll beef in flour mixed with paprika (easiest to do in a plastic bag). Put into an ovenproof casserole dish (enamelled cast-iron or pottery) that will hold ingredients comfortably with not too much extra space. Whizz tomatoes and their juice in a food processor, or crush roughly with a wooden spoon, and add to meat. Add remaining ingredients to casserole and stir. Press a piece of baking paper over contents and cover with lid. Cook in oven for 2 hours. Taste for seasoning. Check if meat is tender and cook longer if necessary.

3 Offer stew with a bowl of yoghurt and maybe a small bowl of pickled dill cucumbers, if desired.

Veal chops in red wine with bacon and mushrooms

Small veal chops from young 'vealers' or bobby calves were always a family favourite, and I still love them. This meat is relatively inexpensive and, when cooked slowly, succulent. The red wine is a surprise as most veal casseroles use white wine, but this dish has always been well received.

1 kg young veal chops
sea salt and freshly ground
    black pepper
½ cup (75 g) plain flour
2 tablespoons olive oil
3 thick rashers rindless smoked streaky bacon,
    cut into 5 mm lardons
2 cloves garlic, finely chopped
1 cup (250 ml) dry red wine
1 generous sprig thyme
1 bay leaf
½ cup Veal Stock or Chicken Stock (see page 134)
200 g button mushrooms
boiled small new potatoes rolled in
    butter and parsley or rice,
    to serve

1 Preheat oven to 180°C.

2 Roll chops in seasoned flour (easiest to do in a plastic bag) and set aside. Gently heat olive oil in an enamelled cast-iron casserole over low heat and sauté bacon until fat has rendered. Remove bacon with a slotted spoon and brown chops in remaining fat, in batches if necessary. Lift chops from casserole and set aside. Sauté garlic for 1 minute. Deglaze casserole with wine, scraping and stirring well. Return chops to casserole, settling them down into the bubbling wine. Scatter bacon into casserole, then drop in thyme and bay leaf. Add sufficient stock to barely cover meat.

3 Cover casserole with lid and cook in oven for 1 hour. Check that chops are nearly tender, then drop in mushrooms and cook for another 30 minutes. Serve with boiled small new potatoes rolled in butter and parsley or rice.

This is one of Italy's best-known dishes, and deservedly so. The most difficult part of the recipe will be obtaining high-quality pale veal. I suggest an Italian butcher. The dish can also be prepared using thin slices cut on the diagonal from a turkey or chicken breast.

4 × 150 g veal scaloppine
12 paper-thin slices prosciutto crudo
12 fresh sage leaves
sea salt and freshly ground black pepper
½ cup (75 g) plain flour
100 g unsalted butter
2 tablespoons olive oil
1 cup (250 ml) dry white wine or
    dry marsala
extra sage leaves, crisped in 40 g butter
    (optional), to serve

1 Cut each scaloppine into 3 pieces. Place a plastic bag over veal and flatten meat gently using a meat mallet or heavy tumbler. Lay a slice of prosciutto on a chopping board and top with a sage leaf, then a piece of veal. Fold ends of prosciutto to enclose the veal. Dip each piece of veal in seasoned flour and shake off excess. Repeat with remaining prosciutto, sage leaves and veal.

2 Heat half the butter and half the olive oil in a large frying pan until foaming. Slip in 6 veal parcels, folded-side down, and brown for 3 minutes on each side, then transfer to a warm plate; do not crowd the pan. Wipe out pan but do not wash it. Heat remaining butter and oil and cook rest of veal. Return all veal parcels to pan and increase heat to high. Pour over wine and let it bubble furiously for a minute. Serve immediately, garnished with extra sage leaves crisped in browned butter, if desired.

Roast lamb and vegetables with rosemary and garlic

When I made this to be photographed I also roasted halved potatoes directly on the oven rack alongside the lamb for one hour. Cooked this way, they develop a crackling exterior that I find irresistible. If you choose to follow suit, omit the potatoes in the Roasted Vegetables with Rosemary and Garlic below.

1 × 1.5 kg leg lamb
sea salt and freshly ground black pepper
extra-virgin olive oil, for drizzling
2 cloves garlic, cut into slivers
2 sprigs rosemary, cut into 4 pieces each
150 ml white wine, for gravy (optional)

ROASTED VEGETABLES WITH ROSEMARY AND GARLIC

4 waxy or all-purpose potatoes, washed, dried
    and halved (or 8–10 small potatoes)
2 onions, cut into wedges
400 g peeled and seeded pumpkin,
    cut into 4 cm chunks
4 chunky carrots, peeled and halved if large
4 parsnips, peeled and halved if large
8 cloves garlic, unpeeled and pierced
    with a fine skewer
¼ cup (60 ml) extra-virgin olive oil
sea salt and freshly ground black pepper
2 tablespoons rosemary leaves

1 Preheat oven to 200°C.

2 To prepare the roasted vegetables, place vegetables and garlic in a large mixing bowl. Pour over olive oil, then season with salt and pepper. Mix through rosemary.

3 Season lamb with salt and pepper and rub with olive oil, then stud with garlic and rosemary and put into a roasting pan. Roast lamb for 15 minutes. Remove lamb from roasting pan and place it directly onto the oven shelf, then tip prepared vegetables into the roasting pan and move around so the vegetables fit compactly in a single layer without too much extra space. Return pan with vegetables to oven shelf underneath lamb (the juices from meat will drip onto vegetables as they cook). Remove lamb after 45 minutes, cover loosely with foil and rest for at least 20 minutes. The vegetables will continue to cook while lamb rests (shake the pan of vegetables once during this time).

4 To make a quick gravy from the pan juices, transfer vegetables to the resting plate, then pour away any fat in the pan. Place roasting pan over high heat, then deglaze with a little wine, scraping up any caught bits and leaving the sauce to bubble and reduce slightly. Strain, then serve gravy with roast lamb and vegetables.

Seven-hour leg of lamb with anchovy and garlic

SERVES 6

Once upon a time this dish was probably cooked in the cooling communal oven in a French village after all the bread had been baked. A relic of the past, one might think, but it fits perfectly into a modern lifestyle. After 20 minutes' preparation the sealed pot can be put into the oven and then left completely untouched for 7 hours. At the end of the cooking time you will have a succulent and most beautifully perfumed piece of meat that slips from the bone at the first touch of a knife.

A 'Frenched' leg of lamb is one from which the butcher has cut off the knobby end of the shank bone and a little of the shank meat to leave a clean bone protruding, which can be grasped for easy carving. A Frenched leg fits more neatly into a closed oval-shaped casserole dish, an essential item for this recipe. Force the meat into the casserole before you start any further preparation, and if the lid does not close completely, choose another pot.

1 × 1.8–2 kg leg lamb, Frenched
(ask your butcher to do this)
4 anchovy fillets, dried on paper towel,
each cut into 3 pieces
3 large cloves garlic, quartered
freshly ground black pepper
sea salt
1 tablespoon olive oil
1 × 200 g piece pork rind with 5 mm
fat attached
2 bouquets garnis (including thyme
sprigs, a fresh bay leaf and a small
piece of celery)
1 cup (250 ml) full-flavoured Veal Stock
or Chicken Stock (see page 134)
1 cup (250 ml) dry white wine
mashed potato, to serve (optional)

1 Preheat oven to 120°C. Select an oval-shaped enamelled cast-iron casserole with a tight-fitting lid that will hold the meat snugly.

2 With the tip of a sharp knife, make 6 deep incisions into each side of lamb. Insert 1 piece of anchovy and 1 sliver of garlic into each incision. Grind pepper over lamb and rub in a little salt.

3 Heat olive oil in a heavy-based frying pan and seal lamb on all sides until a rich golden brown. Put pork rind in selected casserole, fat-side down. Add bouquets garnis and lamb, then pour in stock and wine. Put on lid. (If you are at all unsure of the lid's tight fit, mix some flour and water to a paste and smear it around the edges to seal where the lid fits into the pot.) Stand casserole on a baking tray and transfer to oven. Forget about it for 7 hours.

4 When ready to serve, remove casserole from oven and carefully transfer lamb and pork rind to a hot serving dish. Pour juices into a jug, leave to settle for 5 minutes, then spoon away most of the fat that has risen to the top. Transfer juices to a small saucepan and boil rapidly over high heat until reduced by one-third. Pour juices into a sauceboat. Gently carve meat (it will be very tender and will break up). Cut pork rind into small slivers so that diners can enjoy its succulence. Moisten meat generously with cooking juices and serve with something comforting, such as mashed potato.

Oxtail braised with black olives

One must suck the bones when eating this deliciously sticky braise, so I advise steaming or microwaving some rolled-up, wet cotton face-washers as the Chinese do for fast, effective clean-ups.

3.5 kg oxtail, sawn into sections and trimmed
    of fat (ask your butcher to do this)
sea salt and freshly ground black pepper
plain flour, for dusting
butter, for cooking
olive oil, for cooking
100 ml brandy
1 large onion, diced
4 carrots, diced
1½ cups (375 ml) dry red wine
1 bay leaf
1 sprig thyme
6 cloves garlic, peeled
1 × 6 cm piece fresh or dried orange zest
1 litre stock, tomato juice or water
¾ cup (80 g) pitted black olives
mashed potato, to serve (optional)

1 Preheat oven to 160°C.

2 Roll oxtail in seasoned flour (easiest to do in a plastic bag) and brown well in batches in a frying pan in butter and olive oil. Transfer browned meat to a large enamelled cast-iron casserole. Place dish over low heat and cook for 2–3 minutes. Flame with warmed brandy, shaking dish until flames have died down.

3 Wipe out frying pan and sauté onion and carrot in 1 tablespoon olive oil for 10 minutes. Pour over wine and bubble fiercely. Stir to ensure deglazing is complete, then tip contents of pan over oxtail. Add herbs, garlic, orange zest and stock, juice or water, which should barely cover meat. Cover with buttered baking paper, then put lid on firmly and cook in oven for 2½ hours.

4 Strain sauce from meat into a tall jug and allow fat to rise. Protect meat from drying out by covering it again with the baking paper. Remove fat from sauce. If sauce is too thin, transfer to a small saucepan and boil rapidly over high heat for 2–3 minutes. Pour sauce back over meat, then add olives and continue to cook until oxtail is about to drop from bones, about 45 minutes. (Alternatively, refrigerate braise overnight without degreasing it. The next day, or the day after, remove the fat, which will have solidified, add olives and reheat as above.) Serve with mashed potato, if desired.

Mary was my mother and my mentor. This rabbit pie is a family heirloom, cooked wherever and whenever my family meets. My mother would have used any rabbit caught by my grandpa, and the pie would have had more or less meat in it accordingly – so a wild rabbit of any size will do here. Farmed rabbits were un-heard of in Mum's day, although these days it might be all that is available.

1 wild rabbit
2 litres Chicken Stock (see page 134)
    or water
1 stick celery, chopped
½ carrot, sliced
1 onion, chopped
1 piece lemon zest
1 stalk flat-leaf parsley
1 bay leaf
1 sprig thyme
1 teaspoon black peppercorns
100 g smoked streaky bacon, minced
200 g button mushrooms, sliced
100 g flaked almonds, toasted
1 cup freshly chopped flat-leaf parsley
sea salt and freshly ground black pepper
1 quantity Shortcrust Pastry
    (see page 138)
½ cup (35 g) fresh breadcrumbs
mustard, chutney or pickled fruit,
    to serve

SAUCE
75 g butter
½ cup (75 g) plain flour
3 cups (750 ml) reserved cooking liquid
100 ml pouring cream
juice of 1 lemon
sea salt and freshly ground black pepper

1 Remove kidneys and liver from rabbit and reserve. Simmer rabbit in stock with celery, carrot, onion, zest, herbs and peppercorns until back legs test tender, 1–2 hours. Allow rabbit to cool completely in stock. Remove rabbit. Reduce stock by about one-third by boiling over high heat, then strain and set aside. Strip all meat from carcass and cut into small pieces. Discard bones.

2 Lightly sauté bacon and mushrooms and quickly sear reserved kidneys and liver. Chop kidneys and liver and mix with rabbit meat, bacon, mushrooms and almonds in a bowl. Mix in parsley and season well. Cover with plastic film.

3 To make the sauce, cook butter and flour in a saucepan over low heat to make a roux. Gradually stir in reserved cooking liquid and bring to simmering point. Add cream and lemon juice and simmer for 10 minutes, using a simmer mat to prevent sauce from sticking. Check for seasoning, then add enough sauce to meat to make a creamy, not sloppy, filling. Allow to cool completely.

4 Preheat oven to 200°C.

5 Line a 28 cm × 18 cm × 5 cm lamington tin with pastry (reserve some pastry to make a latticed top) and bake blind for 20 minutes. Remove pastry case from oven and allow to cool. Reduce oven temperature to 180°C. Spoon filling into pastry case (it will be easier to cut squares or wedges if filling is a maximum of 4 cm deep). Scatter top with breadcrumbs and criss-cross strips of pastry over filling. Bake for 15–20 minutes until pastry is well browned. Serve warm or cold with mustard, chutney or pickled fruit.

Egg and bacon pie

Different families have different traditions. When making this pie, our family always kept the eggs whole, whereas other families break the yolks with a fork so that the yolk oozes through the layers of egg white. Sometimes, the pie is topped with puff pastry.

1 quantity Shortcrust Pastry (see page 138)
6 rashers thickly sliced smoked streaky
   bacon, rind removed
2 tablespoons freshly chopped
   flat-leaf parsley
1 teaspoon freshly snipped chives
11 free-range eggs
sea salt and freshly ground black pepper

1 Preheat oven to 180°C. Line a 22 cm flan tin with a removable base with just over half the pastry and chill for 30 minutes. Roll out rest of pastry to make a lid and set aside.

2 Lightly fry bacon and cut into pieces. Scatter two-thirds of the bacon over base of pastry case. Scatter with half the herbs. Break 10 of the eggs, one at a time, into a cup and slip each into pastry case, being careful not to break yolks. Season and add rest of herbs. Carefully add remaining bacon, then cover with pastry lid. Let pastry settle over the hump of each egg, then trim it and seal edges carefully. Whisk remaining egg and a pinch of salt together and brush over pastry. Bake for 35 minutes until a rich gold. Allow to cool before removing from tin. Serve warm or cold.

Eggplant and pork patties

These patties are a great way of combining vegetables with a small amount of meat and have been very successful with young people, who tend to be suspicious of eggplant.

1 eggplant (aubergine) (about 400 g)
200 g spinach leaves, well washed
    and tough stems removed
200 g minced pork (or minced veal
    or beef)
1 clove garlic, finely chopped
100 g fresh ricotta, crumbled
30 g soft breadcrumbs (from
    about 1 thick slice bread)
¼ cup (20 g) grated parmesan
½ teaspoon sea salt
freshly ground black pepper
1 free-range egg
½ cup (35 g) fine fresh breadcrumbs
¼ cup (60 ml) olive oil, for pan-frying
1 cup (250 ml) Fast Basic Tomato
    Sauce (see page 136) or tinned
    chopped tomato (optional)

1 Roast eggplant on a hot barbecue grill plate, turning 2–3 times to roast evenly; it will take about 15 minutes for skin to char and eggplant to feel quite soft. (This can also be done over a gas flame.) Cool a little. Peel charred skin. Halve eggplant lengthways and put into a colander over a baking tray for 20 minutes to catch draining juices. Wrap eggplant with a clean tea towel and gently squeeze. Chop flesh quite finely and put into a large bowl.

2 Half-fill a wok with water and bring to boil. Put spinach into a bamboo steamer over the wok, cover and steam for about 3 minutes. Press spinach in a clean colander with the back of a spoon to extract as much liquid as possible. When cool enough to handle, squeeze in a dry tea towel, then chop quite finely and add to eggplant.

3 Add minced pork, garlic, ricotta, soft breadcrumbs, parmesan, salt, pepper and egg to eggplant mixture and mix very well with clean hands. Fry a tiny ball of mixture to check the salt and pepper (if you can't bring yourself to taste it raw). Cover with plastic film and chill in the refrigerator for at least 30 minutes.

4 Divide mixture into 10 balls and slightly flatten. Roll each in fine breadcrumbs. Heat 2 tablespoons of the olive oil in a large non-stick frying pan over medium heat and, working in batches, gently fry patties for 5 minutes on each side; they will brown very quickly so watch them. Once patties are a rich brown you may prefer to finish cooking them in a frying pan with the fresh tomato sauce or chopped tomato. If not, continue cooking over medium heat until cooked through. Repeat with remaining patties, adding oil to pan as required. Serve.

Braised pork-stuffed cabbage

There are so many recipes for stuffed cabbage. Russians, Poles and Hungarians, as well as the French, all have their own versions. I rather like eating these cold as well as hot. The pork mince should contain about 20 per cent fat for best results. A little bacon could be added if the mince has no fat.

1 cabbage
salt
2 tablespoons extra-virgin olive oil
½ onion, finely chopped
3 cloves garlic, finely chopped
350 g minced pork (with 20% fat)
1 teaspoon sweet paprika
1 tablespoon chopped thyme or oregano
sea salt and freshly ground black pepper
200 g tinned diced tomato
½ cup (125 ml) Veal Stock (see page 134)
    or beef stock
¼ cup (20 g) grated parmesan

1 Turn cabbage upside-down and, with a small, sharp knife, cut a deep circle at the base of the leaves around the core. Remove as many outside leaves as you can. You will need at least 9 perfect leaves, although a few extra will be helpful. Bring a large heavy-based saucepan of lightly salted water to the boil over high heat. Simmer cabbage heart for 10 minutes, then transfer to a bowl of cold water to stop it cooking further. Drain, then squeeze hard in a dry tea towel and finely chop. You need 100 g for the filling. (Store the rest to add to bubble-and-squeak or another dish and use within a few days.) Return saucepan to medium heat.

2 Working in batches, cook cabbage leaves in saucepan of simmering water for 5 minutes. Carefully transfer to a tea towel-lined baking tray. When cool enough to handle, shave heavy central rib flat without cutting it out completely; the aim is to keep the leaf intact but flat so that it is pliable enough to wrap around filling. Set aside.

3 Preheat oven to 180°C.

4 Heat olive oil in a non-stick frying pan over low heat and sauté onion for 8–10 minutes or until very soft. Add garlic and stir for 1 minute, then tip into a mixing bowl. Add minced pork, chopped cabbage, paprika, thyme or oregano, salt and pepper. Mix very well with your hands. Take a small amount of filling and sauté in the frying pan until cooked to check for seasoning, then adjust if necessary.

5 Divide stuffing into 8 balls. Line a 26 cm × 20 cm baking dish with extra cabbage leaves. Wrap each ball in a cabbage leaf and tuck them into the dish, seam-side down. Spoon tomato and stock over and around parcels and scatter over parmesan. Cover with foil and bake for 45 minutes. Remove foil and bake for another 15 minutes to brown tops of cabbage parcels, then serve with baking juices spooned around.

Grilled whiting and French-style peas with crisp sage

The peas combine with the other ingredients to form a sauce that is great served with a delicate fish or meat dish, such as quickly grilled fillets of King George whiting or sautéed escalopes of veal. The fish or meat will not need any other sauce.

8 King George whiting fillets (approximately 700 g), skin-on, pin-boned
40 g butter, melted
sea salt and freshly ground black pepper
2 tablespoons chopped herbs, such as flat-leaf parsley, marjoram and chervil

FRENCH-STYLE PEAS WITH CRISP SAGE
80 g butter, plus 1 teaspoon extra
16 sage leaves
10 lettuce leaves (inner cos, iceberg or other lettuce with a crunchy texture), hard stalk cut away, leaves rolled up and thinly sliced into fine ribbons
4 spring onions, trimmed and very thinly sliced
500 g peas in pod (to yield 160 g shelled peas)
¼ teaspoon salt
⅓ cup (80 ml) water
1 tablespoon chopped flat-leaf parsley

1 To make the French-style peas, heat 40 g of the butter and sage leaves in a large sauté pan over medium heat until leaves are crisp and butter is nut-brown. Quickly scoop out sage leaves and place on a paper towel-lined plate. Wipe out pan.

2 Heat remaining butter in sauté pan over medium heat and drop in lettuce, spring onion, peas, salt and water. Cover tightly and cook for about 10 minutes; peas should be bright green and unwrinkled and lettuce should be quite limp. Taste a pea to see if they need further cooking.

3 Meanwhile, heat an overhead grill. Line grill tray with foil. Brush foil with a little melted butter, then arrange fillets closely together on top. Brush each fillet with remaining butter, then season lightly with salt and pepper and scatter over herbs. Grill fish for 5 minutes or until just cooked through.

4 When peas are tender, add parsley, extra butter and crisp sage leaves. Shake very gently to melt butter. Spoon peas onto hot plates and top with fish fillets, then scatter with sage.

Spiced cauliflower and fish masala

This colourful dish can be served as part of an Indian-inspired meal with a selection of side dishes, or omit the fish and offer it as one of the accompaniments to a Western-style barbecue. It is based on a recipe in the excellent book *Singapore Food* by Wendy Hutton. The cauliflower is quite spicy, so the chilli could easily be omitted or reduced.

¼ cup (60 ml) peanut oil
½ teaspoon mustard seeds
2 tablespoons finely chopped ginger
2 cloves garlic, finely chopped
½ teaspoon cumin seeds
½ teaspoon ground turmeric
1 onion, halved and thinly sliced
400 g trimmed cauliflower florets
220 g tinned chopped tomato
400 g chunky white fish fillets such as blue-eye
   trevalla or hapuku, cut into bite-sized pieces
1 fresh long green chilli, seeded and sliced
½ teaspoon salt
coriander sprigs, to serve

1 Heat oil in a large non-stick frying pan over medium heat. Add mustard seeds and wait a few seconds until they start to pop. Add ginger, garlic, cumin, turmeric and onion and stir for 8 minutes or until the onion is well softened. Add cauliflower and turn until every piece is well coated with spice mixture, then add tomato, fish, chilli and salt. Stir to mix, then cover. Cook for 8–10 minutes, stirring once or twice until cauliflower is just tender. Serve scattered with coriander sprigs.

Coulibiac of salmon with melted butter sauce

SERVES 8–10 AS A MAIN AND 16 AS A STARTER

This recipe is sure to terrify most people by its length alone, but making brioche and making pancakes are pretty basic skills, and poaching fish, cooking rice and boiling eggs are not very challenging, either. As is often the case, a multi-step recipe looks more daunting than it is. This is sure to establish your reputation as an impressive and serious cook!

All preparation can be completed the day before the dinner, except making the brioche. The assembly should be completed about one hour before dinner. If you must assemble several hours before the party, place the assembled loaf in the refrigerator to slow the working of the yeast, but remember to bring the coulibiac out a good hour before you wish to cook it. The dough will need this time to recover and to puff – otherwise your laborious filling will be encased in an unappetising hard crust.

butter, for greasing
6 spring onions, finely chopped
200 g button mushrooms, sliced
1 kg fillet salmon or ocean trout,
    pin-boned
sea salt and freshly ground
    black pepper
2 sprigs flat-leaf parsley
1 sprig dill
100 ml dry vermouth
200 ml dry white wine
1 free-range egg, lightly beaten
    for glazing
chopped dill, to serve

FISH SAUCE
reserved liquid from cooking the fish
150 ml Fish Stock (see
    page 135) or water
60 g butter
60 g plain flour
3 free-range egg yolks
¼ cup (60 ml) pouring cream
sea salt and freshly ground
    white pepper
few drops of lemon juice

DILL CRÊPES
½ cup (75 g) plain flour
1 tablespoon chopped dill
1 tablespoon chopped flat-leaf parsley
1 free-range egg, plus 1 egg yolk, lightly beaten
sea salt and freshly ground black pepper
300 ml milk
30 g butter, melted
clarified butter (see page 140), for cooking

RICE AND EGGS
30 g butter
1 tablespoon finely chopped onion
100 g long-grain rice
350 ml Fish Stock (see page 135) or
    Chicken Stock (see page 134)
sea salt and freshly ground
    black pepper
3 free-range eggs
2 tablespoons chopped flat-leaf parsley

SIMPLE BRIOCHE DOUGH
30 g caster or white sugar
1 cup (250 ml) milk
2 teaspoons dried yeast
6 free-range egg yolks, lightly beaten
3⅓ cups (500 g) plain flour
1 teaspoon salt
150 g soft unsalted butter, chopped

MELTED BUTTER SAUCE
200 g unsalted butter, cut into 6 even pieces
lemon juice, to taste
sea salt and freshly ground black
    or white pepper

1 To cook the fish, preheat oven to 180°C. Butter a baking dish that will hold fish comfortably. Scatter over spring onion and mushroom. Lay fish in the dish, then season and sprinkle with herbs. Pour over vermouth and white wine. Cover with well-buttered foil and bake for 15 minutes; it is only partly cooked at this stage. Lift the fish out with a slice onto a tray, and as soon as you can handle it, remove and discard skin, then scrape away brownish flesh under skin and leave to cool. Cover with plastic film. Strain cooking liquid into a bowl and reserve.

2 To make the fish sauce, measure reserved liquid and add enough fish stock to yield 600 ml. Heat it to simmering point. Melt butter in a saucepan and add flour, stirring well to make a roux, then cook for 3–4 minutes. Gradually whisk in the hot stock, whisk well and bring to simmering point. Simmer for 10 minutes over low heat, then remove from heat. Beat egg yolks with cream, ladle in a little hot sauce, whisk well, then pour back into the pan and return to low heat. Stir for 2–3 minutes to enrich and slightly thicken the sauce; do not allow to boil. Taste for seasoning and adjust with drops of lemon juice; it should be quite thick, smooth and mellow. Press plastic film down on the surface to prevent a skin forming, and reserve.

3 To prepare the dill crêpes, put flour and herbs into a bowl and make a well in the centre. Drop in lightly beaten egg and egg yolk and season with salt and pepper. Add 150 ml of the milk. Gradually mix from centre of well, drawing flour in gradually to avoid lumps. Add remaining milk and whisk well. Leave batter to rest for 2 hours.

4 Add melted butter to crêpe batter and mix well. Heat a well-seasoned 16 cm crêpe pan and grease lightly with clarified butter. Tip in some crêpe batter, swirl to spread, tip off excess and cook for 1–2 minutes. Turn and cook other side quickly. Transfer each crêpe to a plate as you go, separating them with baking paper or foil. (Makes 12 thin crêpes.) Reserve. (If the crêpes have adhered to each other, warm in a 150°C oven for a few minutes so they separate without tearing.)

5 To prepare the rice and eggs, melt butter in a saucepan over low heat and simmer onion until soft and yellow. Add rice and stir until each grain is shiny. Add warm stock, cover and bring slowly to the boil. Stir in salt and pepper to taste, cover rice with a clean, folded tea towel or paper towel and replace lid. Turn heat to lowest possible setting, slip a simmer mat underneath and continue to cook for 12 minutes or until rice is quite tender and all stock has been absorbed. Turn into a bowl and set aside. Hard-boil the eggs. Press through a sieve and mix while warm with the rice, parsley and salt and pepper to taste. Set aside.

6 Start the brioche 3 hours before cooking the coulibiac. Warm the sugar and milk in a pan until just lukewarm. Sprinkle over the yeast and leave for 10 minutes to froth. Add egg yolks to warm yeast/milk mixture. Sift flour and salt into a large bowl, form a well in the centre and pour in milk mixture. Beat well using an electric mixer with a hook. Add softened butter in several lots, beating well after each addition. Continue to beat until dough is shiny and smooth and comes away cleanly from the side of the bowl. Transfer dough to a lightly buttered bowl. Cover with a damp cloth and leave to rise in a warm place for 2–2½ hours. When well risen, knock dough down and proceed to final assembly of the coulibiac.

7 To assemble, butter a large baking tray. Put brioche dough onto a well-floured chopping board and pat into a 30 cm × 15 cm rectangle 1 cm thick. Transfer to the buttered baking tray. Down the centre of the brioche assemble layers in the following order:
- a row of 4 overlapping crêpes
- half the rice and egg mixture
- half the sauce
- half the fish
- an additional 4 overlapping crêpes
- the rest of the rice and egg mixture
- the rest of the sauce
- the rest of the fish
- the last 4 crêpes

8 Preheat oven to 200°C.

9 Brush all exposed brioche with beaten egg. Fold ends up over crêpes and bring sides up to overlap slightly. Pinch and press edges firmly together. Carefully turn roll over so that seam is underneath. Brush whole surface with egg. Leave in a warm place for about 20 minutes to recover from the working and to puff a little. (Remember, it will need longer than this if it has been assembled some hours previously and has been refrigerated.)

10 Bake for 10 minutes, then reduce oven temperature to 180°C and cook for a further 15–20 minutes until the coulibiac looks puffed and golden brown. Leave to rest for 10 minutes to settle before serving.

11 To make the melted butter sauce, bring 1 cm water to a fast boil in a small cast-iron or enamelled frying pan. Whisk 1 piece of butter into the boiling water at a time, lifting the pan and moving it away from the heat for the first piece or two. Then, as the butter takes longer to melt in the lowered temperature, you can finish adding it over the heat; do not stop whisking. Remove from the heat and sharpen with a few drops of lemon juice. Season to taste.

12 Cut coulibiac into thick slices with a serrated knife and hand around separately a jug of melted butter sauce with additional chopped dill.

Sweets

Berry crumbles

There is something very special about the deep crimson juice from raspberries. This crumble is one of my favourite dishes. Try it with blackberries and mulberries too. It deserves to be served with the very best cream.

50 g unsalted butter
400 g raspberries (or mulberries or
    blackberries or a mixture)
⅓ cup (75 g) caster sugar
double or clotted cream, to serve

CRUMBLE TOPPING
⅓ cup (75 g) soft brown sugar
1 teaspoon baking powder
1 teaspoon ground ginger
60 g unsalted butter, chopped
⅔ cup (100 g) plain flour

1 Preheat oven to 200°C.

2 To make the crumble topping, mix sugar, baking powder and ginger in a bowl. In another bowl, crumble butter into flour with your fingertips to make pea-sized pieces, then toss flour mixture with sugar mixture. Set aside.

3 Use some butter to grease four ½ cup (125 ml-capacity) gratin dishes. Divide berries among dishes. Press them down lightly with the back of a spoon. Scatter over sugar. Spoon over crumble topping; it should be no more than 1 cm deep (any extra crumble topping can be put into a suitable container, labelled and frozen, ready for a crumble some other day). Cut remaining butter into small pieces and dot over tops of crumbles. Set dishes on a baking tray with a lip to catch any overflowing juices.

4 Bake crumbles for 15 minutes or until topping is golden and berry juices are bubbling through. Leave crumbles to cool for several minutes before serving with spoonfuls of double or clotted cream.

Fluffy buttermilk pancakes with strawberries and blueberries

These pancakes are the sort often served with maple syrup, whipped butter or honey. I like to include plenty of berries in the batter, then warm extra berries in a pan with butter and maple syrup to spoon over as a delicious sauce.

3–4 free-range eggs (at room
    temperature), separated
60 g unsalted butter, melted, plus
    extra for cooking
2 cups (500 ml) buttermilk
2 cups (300 g) plain flour
1 teaspoon salt
1 teaspoon bicarbonate of soda
400 g strawberries, hulled and sliced
300 g blueberries
maple syrup (optional), to serve

BERRY SAUCE
20 g unsalted butter
1 tablespoon maple syrup
250 g mixed blueberries and
    halved strawberries

1 Preheat oven to 100°C and put a baking dish inside to warm.

2 Put egg yolks into a large mixing bowl. Add melted butter and buttermilk and whisk well. Sift flour, salt and bicarbonate of soda over egg yolk mixture and fold in with a large metal spoon. Stir in berries. The batter should be of a thick, dropping consistency.

3 When ready to cook, whisk egg whites in an electric mixer to soft peaks, then fold into batter with a large metal spoon.

4 Lightly grease a non-stick frying pan with extra butter. Working in batches, ladle in ¼ cup (60 ml) batter per pancake. Cook pancakes until bubbles form on the uncooked side. Flip and cook on the other side, adding a little extra butter if pan seems too dry. Transfer to warm baking dish until all pancakes are cooked.

5 To make the berry sauce, heat butter and maple syrup in a small saucepan over medium heat, then add berries. Cover and cook for 3–4 minutes or until the syrupy juices bubble but the berries still retain some shape.

6 Spoon berry sauce over pancakes and serve at once with a jug of maple syrup, if desired.

Orange chiffon cupcakes

Chiffon cakes are as light as air. The batter cannot sit around so place the cupcake cases inside a muffin tin, preheat the oven to the right temperature and have a large spoon ready to scoop the batter into the paper cases as soon as it is made.

125 g plain flour
½ cup (110 g) caster sugar
½ teaspoon salt
1 teaspoon baking powder
1 teaspoon finely grated orange zest
¼ cup (60 ml) vegetable oil
¼ cup (60 ml) strained orange juice
1½ tablespoons water
3 free-range egg yolks
unsprayed orange blossoms (optional),
    to serve

MERINGUE
4 free-range egg whites (at room
    temperature)
60 g caster sugar
⅛ teaspoon cream of tartar

CREAM CHEESE AND ORANGE ICING
80 g cream cheese
85 g caster sugar
1 teaspoon finely grated orange zest
2 teaspoons strained orange juice

1 Preheat oven to 190°C. Line a 12-hole muffin tin with paper cupcake cases.

2 Sift flour, sugar, salt and baking powder into an electric mixer with a paddle. Mix zest with oil in a small bowl. Mix orange juice with water in another small bowl. With motor running, mix on low speed and gradually add oil/zest mixture, then egg yolks and finally orange juice/water mixture to flour mixture. Stop the machine once or twice to scrape sides and bottom of the bowl with a spatula. Continue beating until batter is just smooth, then scrape into a large bowl.

3 To make the meringue, whisk egg whites in the clean, dry bowl of the electric mixer to soft peaks. With motor running, add sugar and cream of tartar in a steady stream until you have a soft but glossy meringue. Fold meringue into batter speedily but thoroughly with a large metal spoon. Immediately spoon batter into paper cupcake cases. Bake for 18–20 minutes. Transfer muffin tin to a wire rack, then after 1 minute, lift cakes in paper cases out of holes and cool completely on the wire rack.

4 Meanwhile, to make the cream cheese icing, blend cream cheese, sugar and zest in a food processor until smooth and golden. Thin to required consistency with orange juice. Drop a generous blob of icing onto each cooled cupcake and smooth it with the back of a teaspoon, then top with orange blossoms, if using.

Angie's lemon cake

This cake from my friend Angela Clemens is made in minutes in the food processor. Jane Grigson has a very similar recipe in her *Fruit Book*. She adds candied lemon peel to the cake mixture and a tablespoon of gin to the final syrup.

melted butter, for greasing
1⅔ cups (250 g) self-raising flour
pinch of salt
1 teaspoon baking powder
grated zest of 1 lemon
200 g caster sugar
250 g unsalted butter, softened
4 large free-range eggs

TO FINISH
½ cup (110 g) caster sugar
juice of 1 lemon

1 Preheat oven to 160°C. Line a 22 cm springform tin with baking paper. Brush paper and sides of tin well with melted butter.

2 Sift flour, salt and baking powder into a bowl. Pulverise zest and sugar in a food processor, then add softened butter and process until thick and pale. Add eggs and flour mixture alternately in 2 batches, pulsing briefly after each addition. Tip mixture into tin, then smooth top and bake for about 1 hour or until a fine skewer inserted comes out clean.

3 To finish, stir sugar and lemon juice in a small bowl. Cool cake for a few minutes in tin. Spoon over sugary lemon juice while cake is still warm. Release the spring of the tin and cool completely before turning out and serving.

Mum's red devil's cake

This was the cake that was often packed in my school lunchbox. I love its chewy texture and deep-reddish-brown colour. Mum never iced this cake but I suppose you could – it bakes with a bubbly crust on top. The recipe comes from my grandmother's handwritten collection. A note beside the rather odd method advises that this cake will keep indefinitely. That is quite a claim!

125 g unsalted butter, softened
200 g soft brown sugar
2 free-range eggs, separated
½ cup (125 ml) milk
1⅔ cups (250 g) plain flour
1½ teaspoons bicarbonate of soda
1 tablespoon warm water

CHOCOLATE MIXTURE
150 g bittersweet chocolate, chopped
⅔ cup (150 g) soft brown sugar
½ cup (125 ml) milk or buttermilk
few drops of pure vanilla extract
1 free-range egg yolk, lightly beaten

1 Preheat oven to 180°C and butter a 22 cm round springform or square cake tin.

2 To make the chocolate mixture, gently melt chocolate with sugar, milk and vanilla in a saucepan over low heat. When smooth, remove from heat and stir in egg yolk until mixture thickens slightly. Pour through a coarse strainer into a large mixing bowl and allow to cool a little.

3 Cream butter and sugar until pale and fluffy. Beat egg yolks lightly and mix with milk, then add to butter mixture alternately with flour. Pour cooled chocolate mixture into flour mixture and whisk to combine.

4 Dissolve bicarbonate of soda in warm water and stir into mixture. Whisk egg whites until soft peaks form, then fold into mixture. Pour into prepared tin and bake for 1 hour or until a skewer inserted in centre comes out clean. Cool cake on a wire rack for a few minutes, then release the spring. Cool cake completely before cutting.

Easy plum cake

This is a loose interpretation of the plum kuchen enjoyed by my friend Anna during a six-month stay in Frankfurt. It could be made with other stone fruit, although they will not produce the same dramatic effect as plums, which leave deep-purple juice oozing into the cake.

This is a cake to make and eat on the same day. The texture is not as irresistible if the cake has been refrigerated, and the quantity of oozing fruit makes it very vulnerable to spoilage if left at room temperature for more than a day. If your serving plate is ovenproof you can loosely cover the cake with foil and reheat it in a 180°C oven for about 10 minutes to serve as a warm dessert. Individual portions can also be reheated in this way.

90 g unsalted butter, softened,
　　plus extra for greasing
1 cup (150 g) plain flour
1 teaspoon cream of tartar
½ teaspoon bicarbonate of soda
a pinch salt
1 free-range egg
2–3 tablespoons buttermilk or milk
65 g caster sugar
6–8 large ripe plums (preferably
　　purple-fleshed, such as a blood plum),
　　halved, stoned and cut into halves
pure icing sugar, for dusting (optional)
double cream, to serve

STREUSEL MIXTURE
30 g soft brown sugar
½ teaspoon baking powder
½ teaspoon ground cinnamon
⅓ cup (50 g) plain flour
30 g unsalted butter, chopped

1 Preheat oven to 180°C. Grease an 18 cm square cake tin and line base with baking paper, leaving some overhanging to help ease cake out (it can't be inverted onto a wire rack). Otherwise grease a 20 cm springform cake tin.

2 To make the streusel mixture, mix sugar, baking powder, cinnamon and flour in a bowl. Rub in butter so mixture is a bit crumbly and lumpy. Set aside.

3 Sift flour, cream of tartar, bicarbonate of soda and salt into a bowl. Whisk egg with 2 tablespoons of the buttermilk or milk. Cream butter and sugar until pale and thick in a food processor. Tip in flour mixture and pulse to mix quickly. Add egg and buttermilk mixture and process just until you have a smooth batter; it should be a dropping consistency. If it is quite stiff, mix in remaining buttermilk or milk (this will depend on size of egg used).

4 Scrape batter into prepared tin and smooth the top. Press plum halves into batter in rows or circles. Scatter over streusel mixture. Bake for 35–40 minutes or until a skewer inserted in the edges comes out clean (it will still test soft in the middle where plum juice has oozed into cake batter). Cool cake in tin on a wire rack until just warm. Lift cake out, using overhanging baking paper to assist, then transfer to a plate. Carefully lift base of cake with a wide spatula and ease paper out. Dust cake with icing sugar, if desired, and serve with double cream.

Honey madeleines

These delicate cakes look wonderful piled on a Victorian cake plate (the sort that has a pedestal). Madeleine trays, made specifically for these shell-shaped cakes, are available in specialist cookware shops. Each tray usually makes 12 cakes.

110 g unsalted butter
2 teaspoons honey
2 free-range eggs
⅓ cup (75 g) caster sugar
1 tablespoon soft brown sugar
tiny pinch of salt
1 drop pure vanilla extract
90 g plain flour, plus extra for dusting
1 teaspoon baking powder
pure icing sugar, for dusting

1 Melt 90 g of the butter with honey in a saucepan over low heat. Leave to cool. Combine eggs, caster sugar, brown sugar, salt and vanilla in a food processor. Sift in flour and baking powder, then add cooled honey mixture. Leave to rest for at least 1 hour, or even overnight.

2 Preheat oven to 180°C.

3 Barely melt remaining butter and liberally paint 2 madeleine trays with it. Dust with flour, then shake off any excess. Chill. Spoon in batter to two-thirds full and bake for 9 minutes. Cool for 1 minute, then dislodge cakes by sharply rapping edge of tray on workbench. Cool on a wire rack, patterned side uppermost – the madeleines will become crisp on the outside. Dust with icing sugar before serving.

Buttery lemon thyme and vanilla boomerangs

The flavour of these popular shortbread biscuits is given a bit of intrigue by the inclusion of a generous quantity of chopped lemon thyme. Once rolled in icing sugar and allowed to cool completely, the biscuits can be stored in an airtight container for more than a week.

1 cup (150 g) plain flour
30 g caster sugar
100 g ground almonds
1 teaspoon lemon thyme leaves
125 g cold butter, chopped into 4–5 pieces
½ vanilla bean, broken into small pieces
⅔ cup (110 g) pure icing sugar

1 Put flour, sugar, ground almonds and lemon thyme into a food processor and process for a few seconds. With motor running, feed butter quickly through processor tube. Stop machine as soon as mixture forms a dough.

2 Tip dough onto a sheet of foil. Divide dough into two 4 cm-diameter logs. Wrap each one in foil and chill in the refrigerator for 30 minutes.

3 Preheat oven to 180°C.

4 Cut logs into 1 cm-wide slices. Roll each piece between palms of your hands to form a 5–6 cm-long boomerang-shaped crescent. Put crescents onto a baking-paper-lined baking tray, then chill in the refrigerator for 10 minutes.

5 Bake crescents for 15 minutes or until light golden brown. Cool for a few minutes before handling as they are very fragile at this point.

6 Meanwhile, process vanilla bean with icing sugar in washed and dried food processor until vanilla bean is pulverised. Tip vanilla sugar onto a baking tray and gently roll the cooled biscuits in the sugar. (Once completely cold, store in an airtight container. They firm up after 24 hours in their container and are not nearly as fragile.)

Red, ripe strawberries are superb sliced and piled into a hot, buttered shortcake and eaten with thick cream. For individual shortcakes, make the dough as instructed, then dip a scone cutter in flour and cut without twisting the cutter. Put close together onto a baking tray for soft edges, or apart for crisp edges. Bake at 180°C for 10–15 minutes, then split and fill as for a large cake.

1⅔ cups (250 g) self-raising flour
pinch of salt
⅓ cup (75 g) white sugar, plus extra
    for sprinkling
80 g unsalted butter, softened,
    plus extra for spreading
2 free-range egg yolks
2½ tablespoons milk
250 g strawberries, hulled and sliced
pure icing sugar, for dusting
double cream, to serve

1 Preheat oven to 200°C.

2 Mix flour, salt and sugar in a large bowl. Rub butter into flour mixture until it resembles breadcrumbs. Mix egg yolks lightly with milk. Make a well in dry ingredients and add liquid. Work together quickly to make a soft dough. Turn onto a baking tray and form into a 15 cm diameter round. Bake for 15–20 minutes until golden.

3 Leave to cool a little. Mix berries with a little more sugar. Split shortcake widthways and, while still warm, spread base with extra butter. Pile on sliced berries, lightly put on lid, dust with icing sugar and cut into wedges. Offer double cream separately.

Sticky toffee pudding

This pudding has everything going for it: it is delicious, easy to make, requires no fancy equipment and everyone loves it. To make small puddings, pour the batter into individual greased moulds or muffin tins and bake at 180°C for 20 minutes. Pour over sauce and return to oven as for the large pudding.

170 g dates, pitted and chopped
1 teaspoon bicarbonate of soda
300 ml boiling water
60 g unsalted butter
¾ cup (165 g) caster or soft
    brown sugar
2 free-range eggs
170 g self-raising flour
½ teaspoon pure vanilla extract
whipped cream, to serve

TOFFEE SAUCE
400 g soft brown sugar
1 cup (250 ml) double cream
250 g unsalted butter, chopped
1 vanilla bean, split

1 Preheat oven to 180°C and butter a 20 cm square cake tin.

2 Mix dates and bicarbonate of soda. Pour over water and leave to stand.

3 Cream butter and sugar, then add eggs, one at a time, beating well after each addition. Fold in flour gently, then stir in date mixture and vanilla and pour into prepared tin. Bake in centre of oven for 30–40 minutes until cooked when tested with a skewer. Cool for 5 minutes.

4 Meanwhile, to make the sauce, bring all ingredients to a boil in a small saucepan. Reduce heat and simmer for 5 minutes. Remove vanilla bean. Invert cake onto a baking tray or heatproof serving plate. Pour a little sauce over warm pudding and return it to oven for 2–3 minutes so sauce soaks in. Cut pudding into squares and offer remaining sauce and cream separately.

Emily Bell's Christmas puddings

This is my grandmother's Christmas pudding – the best in the world! I have successfully kept cooked puddings for a year in the refrigerator. They were even more delicious the next year. Each pudding will serve six people. You will need to order the suet from your butcher: hopefully he may mince it for you. Packet suet is already mixed with flour and will alter the proportions.

500 g suet (to yield 360 g after grating)
180 g plain flour
2½ cups (205 g) fresh white breadcrumbs
360 g seedless raisins
360 g currants
180 g sultanas
125 g candied peel
180 g dark brown sugar
grated zest of 1 lemon
½ nutmeg, freshly grated
¼ teaspoon salt
2 tablespoons lemon juice
½ teaspoon ground cinnamon
4 free-range eggs
100 ml brandy
600 ml milk, plus more if needed
Custard (see page 138) or ice-cream, to serve

1 Strip as much skin as you can from suet and grate suet on the largest hole of a grater or with the grating disc of a food processor to achieve 360 g. (Measure this very carefully.)

2 Mix all ingredients in a large bowl. (Everyone should have a stir and a wish!) The mixture should be fairly wet. Increase milk a little, if necessary. Refrigerate overnight.

3 Next day, eat a bit to see if it has enough spice for your taste and adjust, if necessary. Pack mixture into two 1 litre-capacity buttered basins, then cover with a disc of baking paper and a double sheet of foil. Tie securely under the rim with a doubled length of kitchen string. Stand each basin on a wire rack inside a stockpot and add boiling water to come two-thirds up their sides. Boil for 6 hours, topping up stockpots as needed with more boiling water. Cool and store in a cool place until Christmas Day.

4 The puddings will take at least 1 hour's boiling on Christmas Day to be really hot, but can boil away for a lot longer. Serve with custard or ice-cream, or flame the turned-out pudding with warmed brandy.

Blueberry and panettone puddings

This is an excellent way to use some of the extra panettone that often lands in households around Christmastime. Panettone is the super-light eggy vanilla-scented loaf beloved of Italians. If you don't have any, use a light egg-based bread or even croissants.

softened butter, for greasing
2 tablespoons caster sugar
4 free-range eggs
100 g crustless panettone or other light
    bread, cut into 5 mm cubes
200 g blueberries
400 ml milk
2 tablespoons raw sugar

1 Preheat oven to 180°C. Grease four 1 cup (250 ml-capacity) gratin dishes well with butter.

2 Whisk together sugar and eggs in a heatproof bowl. Stir panettone and blueberries into egg mixture. Bring milk to scalding point in a small saucepan over high heat. Tip hot milk over panettone and berry mixture and stir to mix. Stand for 5 minutes for panettone to swell. Using a slotted spoon, divide panettone and berry mixture among gratin dishes. Top up with sugar and egg mixture.

3 Stand filled dishes in a roasting pan and pour in boiling water to come halfway up their sides. Bake for 20 minutes or until firm and lightly golden on top. Carefully remove roasting pan from oven and remove puddings. Scatter a little raw sugar on top of each pudding and serve.

Individual pavlovas with passionfruit

These small pavlovas are trickier to bake than one large one to achieve the right combination of crisp outer shell and soft marshmallow inside. The temperatures and times given are correct for my oven. The outer shell should colour only a very little and will feel delicately crisp when lightly tapped with a fingernail.

1 teaspoon cornflour
½ teaspoon white-wine vinegar
2 free-range egg whites,
   at room temperature
½ cup (110 g) caster sugar
½ cup (125 ml) pouring cream
4–6 ripe passionfruit, halved

1 Preheat oven to 150°C.

2 Sift cornflour into a small bowl. Put vinegar into a small container. Whisk egg whites with an electric mixer to form satiny peaks. Dribble in vinegar. With motor running, add one-third of the sugar at a time. Add cornflour and beat once more to combine.

3 Using a large metal spoon, scoop 4 egg-sized portions of the meringue onto a baking-paper-lined baking tray. Bake for 15 minutes, then reduce oven temperature to 120°C and bake for a further 15 minutes. Turn oven off, then hold door ajar with a wooden spoon and leave for 30 minutes. Transfer meringues to an airtight container.

4 Whip cream to stiff peaks. Put a meringue onto each serving plate, then spoon on whipped cream. Leave for at least 30 minutes for cream to soften meringue. Spoon on passionfruit pulp and serve.

Stephanie's quince and browned butter tart

This is one of my signature dishes. The buttery topping oozes into the pastry so that it almost tastes like shortbread, and the dark-pink quince can just be glimpsed through the slightly puffed topping. The tart is best served warm, but is also good cold, and is delicious with really good cream. It keeps very well but is best if not refrigerated. This tart is also delicious made with poached, drained pears or blood plums.

1 quantity Shortcrust Pastry (see page 138)
30 thick slices Poached Quince (see page 139)
double cream, to serve

FILLING
2 free-range eggs
½ cup (110 g) white sugar
1 heaped tablespoon plain flour
125 g unsalted butter

1 Preheat oven to 200°C. Line a 24 cm flan tin with a removable base with pastry and bake blind for 20 minutes. Remove from oven and reduce temperature to 180°C. Leave pastry case to cool, then remove foil and weights. Drain quince well, then arrange slices in a circle around edge and fill in centre with remaining quince.

2 To make the filling, beat eggs and sugar until thick and pale, then add flour. Melt butter and cook until a deep-gold. Add butter to egg mixture and spoon over fruit in pastry case. Bake for 25 minutes or until filling has set. It will look golden brown and be a little puffed but will subside as it cools. Serve warm or cold (but not chilled) with double cream.

Lemon delicious pudding

This pudding is rightly known as delicious. In my house it's a family favourite.

60 g unsalted butter, at room temperature
1½ cups (330 g) caster sugar
3 free-range eggs, separated
¼ cup (35 g) self-raising flour
1½ cups (375 ml) milk
finely grated zest and juice of 2 lemons
pure icing sugar, for dusting
cream, to serve

1 Preheat oven to 200°C. Butter a 2½ cup (625 ml- capacity) baking dish with butter.

2 Cream butter and sugar in an electric mixer until the mixture turns pale. Beat egg yolks into butter and sugar mixture, one at a time. Using a spatula, scrape down sides of the mixing bowl to ensure the whole lot is properly mixed. Add flour and milk alternately, a little at a time, to butter mixture, mixing lightly after each addition until just combined. (Over-mixing will curdle the mixture, which doesn't seem to matter but it can look alarming.) Scrape down sides of bowl again.

3 Using hand-held electric beaters, whisk egg whites to soft peaks.

4 Mix lemon zest and juice into pudding batter. Using a large metal spoon, gently fold in egg whites. Transfer batter into prepared baking dish. Stand baking dish in a roasting pan and pour in enough boiling to come halfway up its sides. Bake for 35–40 minutes until the pudding top is golden and feels springy in the centre when touched.

5 Leave to cool a little. Sprinkle top of pudding with icing sugar and serve with cream.

Rhubarb and scented geranium tart

The combination of rhubarb and rose-scented leaves is lovely.

**1 quantity Shortcrust Pastry
   (see page 138)**
plain flour, for dusting
pouring cream, to serve

ALMOND CREAM
60 g unsalted butter
60 g caster sugar
1 free-range egg
60 g ground almonds

CRUMBLE TOPPING
⅔ cup (100 g) plain flour
50 g soft brown sugar
1 teaspoon baking powder
1 teaspoon ground cinnamon
60 g unsalted butter

RHUBARB FILLING
10 stalks rhubarb, thinly sliced
2 tablespoons soft brown sugar
**3 unsprayed rose-scented geranium leaves,
   washed, dried and finely chopped**

1 Preheat oven to 200°C.

2 Line a 22 cm flan tin with a removable base with pastry and bake blind for 20 minutes. Remove from oven and reduce temperature to 180°C. Leave pastry case to cool, then remove foil and weights.

3 Meanwhile, to make the almond cream, cream butter and sugar in a food processor. Add egg and pulse, then add ground almonds and pulse to combine. Set aside.

4 To make the crumble topping, mix flour, brown sugar, baking powder and cinnamon in a bowl. Rub in butter using your hands so that the mixture is quite lumpy.

5 For the filling, mix rhubarb and brown sugar in a bowl, then add geranium leaves.

6 Cover pastry case with almond cream, then top with rhubarb filling and scatter over crumble mixture.

7 Bake for 20–30 minutes until golden brown. Remove tart from oven. Leave to settle for a few minutes. Serve warm with a small jug of cream alongside.

Lemon crêpes

Crêpes seem to be everyone's favourite treat and they are so simple to make. You need to allow two hours for the batter to rest in the refrigerator before cooking.

1 cup (150 g) plain flour
pinch of salt
2 free-range eggs
1½ cups (375 ml) milk, plus ½ cup (125 ml) extra,
    as needed
30 g unsatled butter, melted and cooled,
    plus extra for cooking
juice of 2 lemons
½ cup (110 g) caster sugar, plus extra
    for sprinkling

1 Sift flour and salt into a large bowl and make a well in the centre. Whisk eggs and milk together lightly, then add cooled melted butter. Tip egg and butter mixture into the well in the flour and gradually fork in the flour. Whisk until a smooth batter forms. Refrigerate for 2 hours before cooking. (The consistency of the rested batter should be like cream. If too thick, add a little more milk.)

2 Preheat oven to 120°C and put a baking tray inside to keep warm.

3 Grease a frying pan with butter, then heat over high heat. Spoon a ladleful of batter into the pan and immediately lift and tilt the pan so batter flows evenly all over the base. Place the pan flat on the stove again, reduce heat to medium and leave for 1 minute. Shake the pan to ensure the crêpe is not sticking and flip it over until cooked. Transfer to baking tray in oven. Continue until all batter is used, adding extra butter to the pan as needed.

4 Drizzle each crêpe with lemon juice, sprinkle with caster sugar and roll up tightly. Sprinkle with more caster sugar, if desired, then serve.

Grape, ginger and yoghurt brûlée

This delicious and incredibly simple dessert relies on using the right-shaped dishes (shallow) and an efficient overhead griller. The yoghurt used must be thick!

350 g seedless red or green grapes,
   stems removed
200 ml Greek-style yoghurt (see page 140)
¼ cup (55 g) soft brown sugar
1 teaspoon ground ginger or cinnamon

1 Pack one-quarter of the grapes really tightly in a single layer into each of four ½ cup (125 ml-capacity) gratin dishes; they will nearly fill the dishes. Spoon yoghurt over, then smooth and press it around grapes with the back of a teaspoon. You are aiming for a smooth surface, just glimpsing the dark shapes beneath. Chill filled dishes in the refrigerator for 1 hour (or even overnight).

2 Preheat overhead griller to maximum.

3 Mix brown sugar and ginger or cinnamon, ensuring there are no small lumps in sugar. Sprinkle an even layer of sugar mixture over yoghurt and smooth with the back of a teaspoon until no yoghurt is visible.

4 Place gratin dishes on a baking tray and slide under griller, then watch carefully. In less than 1 minute the sugar will caramelise and start to bubble. Remove baking tray and allow gratins to settle; don't try to eat this dessert until sugar has stopped bubbling as it will be very hot!

Golden syrup dumplings

This old-fashioned recipe has proved popular with a new generation. The dumplings are poached in the syrup and swell to at least double their uncooked size so it is most important that the pan selected is deep and has a lid.

2 free-range eggs
2½ tablespoons milk
1 tablespoon plain flour
225 g self-raising flour
40 g unsalted butter, softened,
    plus extra for greasing
pouring cream, to serve

SYRUP
juice of ½ lemon
2 cups (500 ml) water
175 g soft brown sugar
¼ cup (90 g) golden syrup
40 g unsalted butter

1 Preheat oven to 120°C. Grease a 6 cup (1.5 litre-capacity) baking dish with a butter and place in the oven to keep warm.

2 To make the syrup, pour lemon juice into a large deep frying pan or sauté pan, then add water, brown sugar, golden syrup and butter. Stir over low heat until butter has melted and sugar has dissolved. Increase heat to medium and bring the syrup to the boil, then immediately remove pan from heat and set aside until needed.

3 To make the dumplings, put eggs and milk into a small bowl and whisk until well combined. Put plain flour into another small bowl. Sift self-raising flour into a large bowl. Using your fingertips, rub in softened butter. Make a well in the centre of flour mixture, then tip in egg mixture. Gently stir until all ingredients are combined. Working in batches and using fingers dipped into bowl of plain flour to stop dough from sticking, roll walnut-sized pieces of dough into small dumplings, placing each one on a plate.

4 Return pan of syrup to simmering point over medium heat, stirring to heat evenly. Carefully add dumplings, quickly cover and cook for 10 minutes without lifting the lid. Check dumplings are cooked – they should look well-risen and fluffy. Carefully lift dumplings out of syrup with a slotted spoon and into warm serving dish or individual bowls. Pour syrup over dumplings.

5 Serve dumplings with a jug of pouring cream offered alongside.

Orange crème caramels

I just had to slip in a recipe here for everyone's favourite dessert. It is best to make this one or two days in advance as more caramel will flow when the custards are turned out to serve.

1 cup (220 g) white sugar
½ cup (125 ml) hot water
1 long strip orange zest
1½ cups (375 ml) milk
2 free-range eggs, plus 2 egg yolks
2 tablespoons caster sugar

1 Make a dark caramel by dissolving sugar in the hot water in a saucepan over medium heat. Carefully divide caramel among four 150 ml-capacity soufflé dishes, turning to coat sides and bases.

2 Preheat oven to 160°C.

3 Put orange zest and milk into a saucepan and bring very slowly to scalding point over low heat. Lightly whisk together eggs, egg yolks and caster sugar, then strain the orange-scented milk into the bowl. Mix gently, then pour evenly into the soufflé dishes.

4 Put filled soufflé dishes into a baking dish, then add boiling water to come halfway up sides of soufflé dishes. Bake for 25–30 minutes or until just set; check after 20 minutes. Leave to cool, then chill in refrigerator for at least 8 hours before turning out.

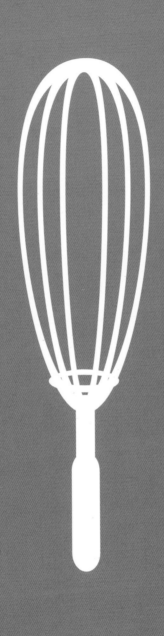

Basics

Chicken stock

1–2 fresh chicken carcasses, chopped
500 g chicken wings
2 chicken gizzards, cleaned (if available)
1 onion, sliced
1 carrot, sliced
1 leek, sliced
1 stick celery, sliced
6 mushrooms, chopped
1 piece lemon zest
1 tomato, peeled, halved and seeded
1 bay leaf
1 sprig thyme
a few stalks flat-leaf parsley
6 black peppercorns

1 Put chicken bones, wings and gizzards, if using, into a stockpot and cover generously with cold water. Bring to simmering point and skim the surface well. Add remaining ingredients. Adjust heat to maintain a very gentle simmer and simmer for 4 hours. Strain stock and allow to cool. Remove any fat that has risen to the surface. Reduce stock to concentrate its flavour, if desired. Refrigerate for 2–3 days, or freeze for up to 3 months.

Veal stock

1 kg veal shanks, sawn into
    small pieces
1 kg beef brisket, sawn into
    small pieces
1 pig's trotter, sawn in half
2 tablespoons olive oil
3 onions
6 cloves garlic, crushed
2 carrots, sliced
2 leeks, sliced
2 sticks celery, sliced
6 mushrooms, chopped
2 large tomatoes, halved widthways
1 bay leaf
1 sprig thyme
a few black peppercorns

1 Preheat oven to 200°C. Put all meat into a baking dish and sprinkle with oil. Roast for 20 minutes, then turn meat and roast for another 20 minutes – during this time it will become golden brown. Slice 2 of the onions and add to baking dish with garlic and all vegetables, except tomato. Return to oven. While vegetables and meat are browning, cut remaining unpeeled onion in half widthways. Fry onion and tomato halves, cut-side down, in a lightly oiled heavy-based frying pan until cut sides are very dark.

2 Remove bones, meat and vegetables from baking dish, put into stockpot and add onion and tomato halves. Cover generously with cold water, then bring to simmering point and skim the surface very well. When no more scum rises, add herbs and peppercorns and maintain a bare simmer for 8 hours. Strain and allow to cool, then remove any fat that has risen to the surface. Boil to reduce or concentrate the flavour, if desired, and refrigerate for 2–3 days, or freeze for up to 3 months.

Fish stock

heads and bones of 2 flathead
1 onion, sliced
1 carrot, sliced
1 leek, sliced
1 stick celery, sliced
3 stalks flat-leaf parsley
1 bay leaf
1 generous sprig thyme
6 black peppercorns
150 ml dry white wine

1 Wash bones well, scraping away any blood, and cut out and discard gills. Chop bones into a few pieces. Put bones and all other ingredients into a stockpot and stir. Cover well with cold water and bring slowly to simmering point, then skim the surface. Simmer for 20 minutes. Have ready a strainer lined with damp muslin over a large bowl. Ladle stock through muslin, then allow to cool. Refrigerate for 2 days, or freeze for up to 3 months.

Trimmed and cooked artichoke hearts

2 lemons
4 globe artichokes
1 litre Chicken Stock (see opposite) or water

1 Have ready a bucket or basin of cold water with the juice of 1 lemon squeezed into it. Have another halved lemon at the ready.

2 Using disposable kitchen gloves, start pulling off and discarding dark outer leaves of artichoke until leaves are uniformly pale. Hold artichoke on its side on a workbench and use a serrated knife to carefully cut off top half. Rub remaining artichoke with cut lemon. Use a paring knife to trim artichoke base and cut away nubs where discarded leaves were attached until you have a smooth cream-coloured surface. Don't cut too deeply as this the best bit – the heart. Rub quickly with lemon.

3 Either dig into centre of artichoke with a sharp teaspoon to remove any prickly, pointy, pink-tinged leaves and underneath the choke (tuft of inedible fibrous matter), or halve the artichoke so the prickly leaves and choke are exposed, then remove them. Rub with lemon and drop hollowed hearts into acidulated water. Repeat with remaining artichokes.

4 Immediately transfer prepared artichokes to a saucepan of simmering chicken stock or water and simmer for about 10 minutes until barely tender. Cool in liquid for a few minutes, then lift out with a slotted spoon to cool (store artichokes in cooled cooking liquid to prevent discolouration). They are now ready to use in a salad or to sauté.

Fast basic tomato sauce

⅓ cup (80 ml) extra-virgin olive oil
1 onion, finely chopped
1 fresh bay leaf
500 g ripe tomatoes, cored and
    roughly chopped
2 cloves garlic, finely chopped
8 sprigs basil, oregano or mint
sea salt and freshly ground black pepper
    (or a shake of chilli flakes)
extra freshly torn herbs (optional),
    to serve

1 Heat olive oil in a large non-stick frying pan over medium heat, add onion and bay leaf, then cover and cook for 5 minutes or until onion is well softened but hardly coloured. Uncover and add tomato, garlic and herbs. Cook over medium heat, stirring frequently, for 10 minutes or until tomato has collapsed. Add salt and pepper or chilli flakes to taste.

2 Set up a food mill fitted with a medium disc resting comfortably over a mixing bowl. Carefully pour tomato mixture into food mill. Turn handle to press out all the good stuff, leaving skins and seeds behind. Lift food mill away from bowl and scrape any mixture in bottom of disc into bowl. Season with salt and pepper. Scatter with extra herbs, if using, just before sauce is served.

Sauce ravigote

yolks from 4 hard-boiled eggs
2 tablespoons capers, rinsed, dried
    and chopped
1 tablespoon finely chopped French
    tarragon leaves
¼ cup (3 tablespoons) snipped chives
⅓ cup (4 tablespoons) finely chopped
    flat-leaf parsley
½ cup (125 ml) extra-virgin olive oil
1 tablespoon red-wine vinegar
sea salt and freshly ground black pepper

1 Push hard-boiled egg yolks through a fine-mesh sieve into a bowl, then add remaining ingredients, except salt and pepper, and mix gently (do not use a food processor). Check and adjust seasoning.

Mayonnaise

3 free-range egg yolks
pinch of salt
1 tablespoon lemon juice or
    white-wine vinegar, plus
    extra as needed
300 ml olive oil
freshly ground white pepper
    or Tabasco

1 Choose a comfortable bowl and rest it on a damp cloth, so it cannot slip around. Work egg yolks with salt and lemon juice or vinegar for a minute until smooth. Gradually beat in olive oil using a wooden spoon or a whisk, adding the first few tablespoons one at a time and beating very well after each. After one-third of the oil has been added, the rest can be added in a thin, steady stream, beating all the while. (This is easiest to do if you have a helper to pour while you beat.) Taste for acidity and adjust with drops of lemon juice, salt and pepper or Tabasco. Refrigerate with plastic film pressed on the surface to prevent a skin forming. Return to room temperature before using, then stir to ensure mayonnaise is smooth and skin-free.

Beer batter

1 cup (150 g) plain flour
½ cup (125 ml) milk
½ cup (125 ml) beer
1 free-range egg (at room
    temperature), separated

1 Put flour into a medium mixing bowl. In another bowl, whisk milk, beer and egg yolk together. Make a well in flour, tip in beer mixture and whisk until smooth. Just before you are going to start frying, whisk egg white with hand-held electric beaters to form stiff peaks and fold into batter with a large metal spoon. Proceed with the recipe.

Eggwhite batter

1⅔ cups (250 g) plain flour
1 teaspoon salt
½ cup (125 ml) olive or vegetable oil
1½ cups (375 ml) warm water
2 free-range egg whites

1 Put flour and salt into a bowl and make a well. Mix oil with warm water and tip into bowl. Whisk batter until smooth. Leave for at least 1 hour, then beat egg whites until stiff and fold into batter with a large metal spoon. Use immediately.

Shortcrust pastry

180 g unsalted butter
240 g plain flour, plus extra
  for dusting
pinch of salt
¼ cup (60 ml) water

1 Remove butter from refrigerator 30 minutes before making pastry. Sift flour and salt onto a marble pastry slab or workbench. Chop butter into smallish pieces and toss lightly in flour. Lightly rub to partly combine. Make a well in centre and pour in water. Using a pastry scraper, work water into flour until you have a very rough heap of buttery lumps of dough. Using the heel of your hand, quickly smear pastry away from you across the workbench. It will combine lightly. Gather together, then press quickly into a flat disc and dust with a little flour. Wrap pastry in plastic film and refrigerate for 20–30 minutes. When required, roll out pastry, dusting generously with flour as necessary. Line tin and proceed with recipe.

Custard

Use half milk and half pouring cream for a richer result.

2 cups (500 ml) milk
1 vanilla bean, split
5 free-range egg yolks
½ cup (110 g) caster sugar

1 Bring milk and vanilla bean to simmering point in a heavy-based saucepan. In a bowl, whisk egg yolks with sugar until light and foamy, then whisk in warm milk. Return to rinsed-out pan and cook over medium heat for least 10 minutes, stirring constantly with a wooden spoon, until mixture thickens and coats back of spoon. (If you have a sugar thermometer, 82–85°C is the temperature for a properly thickened custard.) Immediately strain into a cold bowl, then whisk in some vanilla seeds from the split pod. Serve warm or cold.

Poached quince

6 quinces, washed
1 vanilla bean
juice of 1 lemon

LIGHT SUGAR SYRUP
1.5 litres water
3 cups (660 g) white sugar

1 To make the sugar syrup, put water and sugar into a large heavy-based saucepan and stir over low heat until sugar has dissolved; the syrup should barely move during this process.

2 Preheat oven to 150°C. Peel quinces, then cut into quarters or sixths. Cut out cores and tie loosely in a piece of muslin. Put quinces into a large enamelled cast-iron casserole with vanilla bean, lemon juice and muslin bag, then add enough syrup to cover the fruit. Cover tightly and bake for at least 4 (and up to 8) hours until quince is deep red. Do not stir.

3 Cool and serve either on its own or as part of an autumn compote with poached pear and sliced orange, or in a fruit crumble. Split vanilla bean and scrape seeds into quince syrup. (Extra syrup can be refrigerated in an airtight container for a week or frozen.)

Glossary

Cartouche
A piece of baking paper cut or torn to fit the inside diameter of a saucepan or pot so that it settles directly over the food to prevent evaporation, often of braising juices or a poaching syrup.

Clarified butter
Butter heated until the milk solids fall to the bottom of the pan and the clear butter oil can be spooned off. Clarified butter is less likely to burn when heated than regular butter, yet it still retains the true taste of butter.

Fresh mozzarella
The standard-sized balls of fresh, white mozzarella are a little larger than a golf ball. Smaller sizes are sold as 'bocconcini' and even smaller, as 'milk cherries'.

Garlic croûtons
To make, cut 1 loaf day-old sourdough bread into 2 cm-thick slices, remove crusts and cut or tear into 2 cm cubes. Pour ¼ cup (60 ml) extra-virgin olive oil into a bowl and drop in 2 cloves crushed garlic. Add bread and toss well to mix and moisten. Spread on a baking tray in a single layer, leaving crushed garlic in bowl. Bake bread at 180°C for 15 minutes or until golden brown and crusty on the outside but still a bit soft in the middle, shaking the tray halfway through cooking. Tip croûtons back into bowl with garlic and leave to cool. Use immediately or store in an airtight container for a few days (toss in a dry frying pan to warm through before serving).

Greek-style yoghurt
This has approximately 10 per cent butterfat and less whey than other styles of yoghurt.

Pearl barley
This is barley that has had the external husk or bran removed. While still taking some time to cook it is speedier than 'pot barley', which has not been 'pearled'.

Ricotta salata
This is a firm yet creamy, pressed and lightly salted ricotta that has a lovely sharp, lemony flavour. Available from Italian-owned delicatessens.

Sterilised jars
To sterilise jars, wash them in hot, soapy water and then rinse them in hot water. Put into a stockpot of boiling water for 10 minutes and then drain upside down on a clean tea towel. Dry thoroughly in an oven set at 150°C. Remove the jars from the oven to fill them while still hot. Once jars have been removed from the oven, avoid any contact with their interior surfaces.

Shrimp paste
A very powerful paste from fermented prawns, it has a pungent smell but adds a wonderful subtlety to many Asian dishes. It has many local names, among them *trasi*, *blachan* and *kapi*.

Vino cotto (or 'vincotto' – literally 'cooked wine')
A relative newcomer to food shelves across Australia, this condiment has been used in Italy for a long time. This magical ingredient is both sweet and sour. It is made by reducing cooked grape must (the residue after pressing) until thick and syrupy. Vino cotto can be used in marinades, sauces, to baste meat before grilling or to brush onto grilled vegetables.

Index

LANTERN

Published by the Penguin Group
Penguin Group (Australia)
707 Collins Street, Melbourne, Victoria 3008, Australia
(a division of Pearson Australia Group Pty Ltd)
Penguin Group (USA) Inc.
375 Hudson Street, New York, New York 10014, USA
Penguin Group (Canada)
90 Eglinton Avenue East, Suite 700, Toronto, Canada ON M4P 2Y3
(a division of Pearson Penguin Canada Inc.)
Penguin Books Ltd
80 Strand, London WC2R 0RL, England
Penguin Ireland
25 St Stephen's Green, Dublin 2, Ireland
(a division of Penguin Books Ltd)
Penguin Books India Pvt Ltd
11 Community Centre, Panchsheel Park, New Delhi – 110 017, India
Penguin Group (NZ)
67 Apollo Drive, Rosedale, North Shore 0632, New Zealand
(a division of Pearson New Zealand Ltd)
Penguin Books (South Africa) (Pty) Ltd
24 Sturdee Avenue, Rosebank, Johannesburg 2196, South Africa

Penguin Books Ltd, Registered Offices: 80 Strand,
London, WC2R 0RL, England

First published by Penguin Group (Australia), 2012

10 9 8 7 6 5 4 3 2 1

Text copyright © Stephanie Alexander 2012

Photographs copyright © Earl Carter 2012
(pages 25, 27, 28, 31, 59, 61, 65, 66, 69, 73, 75,
86, 89, 99, 100, 105, 109, 111, 112, 119, 131)

Photographs copyright © Mark Chew 2012
(pages 2, 9, 10, 13, 15, 16, 19, 21, 22, 35, 37, 39, 40, 43, 45, 47, 51,
53, 55, 56, 70, 79, 80, 83, 85, 93, 94, 96, 103, 106, 115, 117, 127)

Photographs copyright © Simon Griffiths 2012
(pages 32, 121, 122, 125, 128, 141)

Design by Lantern Studio © Penguin Group (Australia)
Typeset in Alright Sans and Adobe Caslon
by Post Pre-press Group, Brisbane, Queensland
Colour reproduction by Splitting Image, Clayton, Victoria
Printed in China by Everbest Printing Co Ltd

National Library of Australia
Cataloguing-in-Publication data:

Alexander, Stephanie, 1940-
Stephanie Alexander / Stephanie Alexander.

ISBN: 9781921383137 (pbk.)

Lantern cookery classics.
Includes index.

Cooking.

641.5

penguin.com.au/lantern

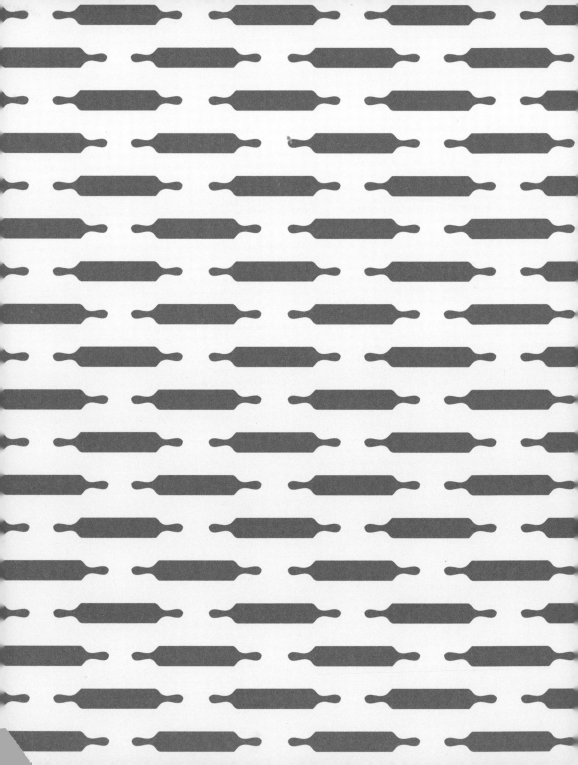